Jews in the Great War:
Family Histories Retold

The Jewish Genealogical Society
of Los Angeles

Exhibit curated, and publication edited, by
Lois Ogilby Rosen

A project of the
International Association of Jewish Genealogical Societies
(IAJGS)
presented at
Salt Lake City 2014

**A gift from the
Jewish Genealogical
Society of Los Angeles**

JGSLA.ORG

Questions regarding this document should be addressed to:
Jewish Genealogical Society [Los Angeles]
P.O. Box 55443
Sherman Oaks, CA 91413
president@jgsla.org

ISBN 978-1-329-40942-2

Foreword

The collection memorialized in this book is a permanent record of the exhibit of the World War I stories submitted by members of IAJGS societies and displayed at the 34th Annual IAJGS Conference on Jewish Genealogy, held in Salt Lake City, Utah. The conference was scheduled to begin on July 28th, 2014, which was pointed out by Jan M. Allen to be the 100th anniversary of the start of World War I. As such, the program was arranged to commemorate this significant anniversary, as an event with tremendous impact on virtually all of our ancestors. The exhibit grew from the determination of the program theme. Jewish genealogists were asked to supply pictures of their family members and to write their stories.

This permanent collection of those materials is intended to commemorate each of those family members whose stories and pictures were submitted.

Special thanks to Lois Ogilby Rosen, who curated the exhibit, and followed that excellent work by producing this permanent record of that exhibit. Huge thanks to the Jewish Genealogical Society of Los Angeles which has agreed to support this publication. Thanks to the IAJGS for agreeing both to the Exhibit, and to the production of this commemorative volume.

Most of all, thanks to the submitters, who shared their ancestors' pictures and stories, to do what we genealogists do, which is to discover and remember the past, and our family members who were so impacted by these horrific events. The lives lived in that era continue to resound in the descendants and families of those individuals.

Sandra L. Malek
President, JGSLA
Program chair, 34th annual IAJGS conference on Jewish Genealogy

Introduction

What experiences did Jews have in World War I? How were they treated by the armies and countries they served? What were their allegiances? Various sources claim that about 140,000 Jews fought in the German and Austrian forces, about 350,00 fought for Russia, about 20,000 for the British and French, and about 250,000 for the U.S. In addition, Palestinian Jews fought with the British Army. It may have been rare for a Jew to be a high-ranking Allied officer, or even trained as a pilot. However, Jews held many coveted positions in the German and Austrian forces. And yet Jews in England, Canada and the U.S. paved a pathway to assimilation by their service, while Jews in Europe subsequently suffered greatly, in spite of having served their countries. We asked Jewish genealogists to tell a story about how their family was affected by the Great War. The stories are varied and compelling. There are tales of brothers and cousins fighting on opposing sides, immigrants escaping conscription in one army only to be drafted in another, and families surviving one war unable to escape the next. I thank the submitters for sharing their stories, and IAJGS and JGSLA for supporting this project.

Lois Ogilby Rosen

Statement from IAJGS

The International Association of Jewish Genealogical Societies (IAJGS) applauds the production of this book by its member society, The Jewish Genealogical Society of Los Angeles (JGSLA), and the exhibit curated by Lois Ogilby Rosen, Board member of JGSLA. The exhibit was well-received by attendees at the 34th annual conference, and the information gathered through submissions of many and diverse genealogists is worthy of preservation. Thanks to JGSLA for ensuring the preservation of these materials, thanks to the submitters of these historical materials, and thanks to Lois Ogilby Rosen and Sandra L. Malek who brought the venture together.

Marlis Humphrey
President, IAJGS

Table of Contents

Notes

 World War I participant

 Perished in Shoah

Family trees prepared by Lois Ogilby Rosen

Henry Bader

British Army
serving in France

Bader
Family Tree

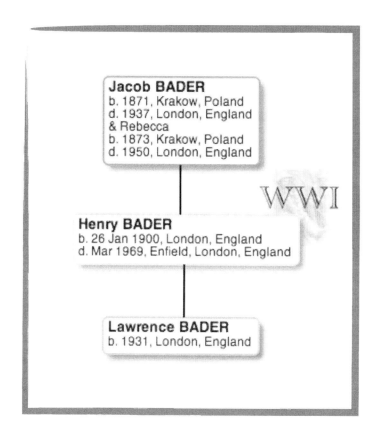

Jacob BADER
b. 1871, Krakow, Poland
d. 1937, London, England
& Rebecca
b. 1873, Krakow, Poland
d. 1950, London, England

WWI

Henry BADER
b. 26 Jan 1900, London, England
d. Mar 1969, Enfield, London, England

Lawrence BADER
b. 1931, London, England

My Father's
First World War Experiences

Lawrence Bader

My father, Henry Bader, was born on 26 January 1900. When he was 15 years old, he volunteered for the Army. I have seen a copy of his signing-on declaration when he gave his age as 19 – must have been quite a lad! He was inspired to volunteer partly out of a sense of patriotism and partly because he didn't want to start work as an apprentice in his father Jacob Bader's chain of ladies hairdressing establishments in London. He was sent to France where he spent three years in the trenches, mainly I believe, as a Company runner, delivering battle-time messages from trench to trench.

He didn't speak much after the war about his experience but I know he had a terrible time – I once discovered a black bound book on a shelf forbidden to me, full of illustrations of dead and mutilated corpses lining the bottom of flooded trenches. After the War in 1918, Henry Bader's father looked forward to seeing his son return to England to start his ladies hairdressing apprenticeship. But Henry Bader had other ideas – he was too fired up by his wartime experiences to want anything to do with ladies' hair. So in order to delay his return, he joined the French Fire Brigade in Calais, France. He rose to the rank of Pompier Premier Classe, but in 1921 there was a very rainy summer and fires were few and far between. He was made redundant.

"Good" his father, Jacob Bader, said. "Now Henry will come home." But Henry Bader was still reluctant to turn his hand to ladies hairdressing and in 1921 he joined the Royal Air Force. He was trained as a bomb-aimer and navigator and was sent to Baghdad where the UK had responsibilities. He flew every day from Baghdad to Basra and returned to deliver forces' mail. He sat in the rear seat of an open two-seater bi-plane. The pilot for his eighteen-month service was T.E. Lawrence, known as Lawrence of Arabia. Lawrence of Arabia was an English First World War hero, known worldwide and the subject of a film starring Peter O'Toole and Omar Sharif and he too was reluctant to give up his life of adventure and return to England.

But eventually Henry Bader had to return to England and he reluctantly joined his father's ladies hairdressing shops. In 1931, I arrived, and I was named Lawrence to commemorate my Father's brush with fame. I was never very keen on the name Lawrence but things could have been worse, after all he might have flown with Amelia Earhart. Eventually, by 1931 Henry Bader became the owner of three ladies hairdressing salons but always remembered his Army/Fire Brigade/Air Force years.

Israel Benveniste

From Rhodes to USA

My Father Remembers World War I and the Balkan War

Arthur Benveniste

My father, Israel Benveniste, was born on the Island of Rhodes in December of 1900. At the time of his birth, the island was part of the Ottoman Empire. During the Balkan War, 1912-1913, Italy took Rhodes and the Dodecanese Islands.

In 1912 the Balkan War broke out. It was a precursor of World War I. Bulgaria, Greece, Montenegro and Serbia attacked and annexed much of the Ottoman possessions in the Balkans. Italy was not officially part of the war, but it took advantage of the Ottoman preoccupation with the war to annex the island possessions.

The Balkan War saw the first use of aircraft in war. My father recalled seeing Italian bi-planes flying low over the island and dropping what appeared to be small hand grenades. These "bombs" did very little damage, but one did explode near the kitchen of a relative and she was cut by flying pieces of crockery. Apparently, this was the only casualty. The Turks fired rifles at the Italian planes, but my father could see no damage done.

World War I broke out the following year. Italy joined the war, on the side of the Allies, in 1915. In 1916, my father emigrated to the United States. He, along with a few other young men from Rhodes, managed to book passage aboard the *Vasilis Constantinides*, a Greek ship.

During their passage across the Atlantic, as my father told me, a German submarine surfaced and boarded the Greek ship. The Germans ordered the Greek captain to deliver two of the passengers to them. The two men were brought forward and turned over to the Germans. The Germans forced them to board the submarine which then sailed away with their prisoners.

The *Vasilis Constantinides* landed in New York on June 14, 1916. Going through immigration, my father claimed to be 17 years old. As a result, later the following year, when the US entered the war, my father's documents indicated that he was 18 years old and eligible for the draft. However, though he carried an Italian passport, he had been born an Ottoman citizen. The U.S. government determined that, since the Ottoman Empire was fighting alongside the Central Powers, my father was an enemy alien. Because of this little quirk of bureaucracy, my father was ineligible for the draft and he did not serve in the Great War.

Manfred Bock

German Army
Anti-aircraft Unit
Rottweil, Germany

My Grandfather in the German Army

Marion Davies

My grandfather Manfred Bock , was born on 28 May 1882 in Frankfurt am Main. Before the war Manfred wanted to become an officer. He was well known in Frankfurt for having had a question raised in the Reichstag (around 1910). This was even mentioned in the personal song composed on the occasion of his wedding in June 1911. The result of this question was negative.

Manfred volunteered on the first day of World War I. He was based in an anti-aircraft unit in Rottweil, Germany.

He had his own horse in the Army (see photograph). My mother, born in 1919, was named by her siblings Lieselotte, after the horse!

Manfred managed to get a visa to come to England in the summer of 1939. He was only allowed to bring £10.

Samuel L. Brenner

American serving in France

The Patriots

Samuel Brenner's wife Rose and daughters
Josephine, Norma and Florence

Beatrice Benton
(Beatrice Brenner)
September 14, 1917
Cincinnati Post

Brenner Family Tree

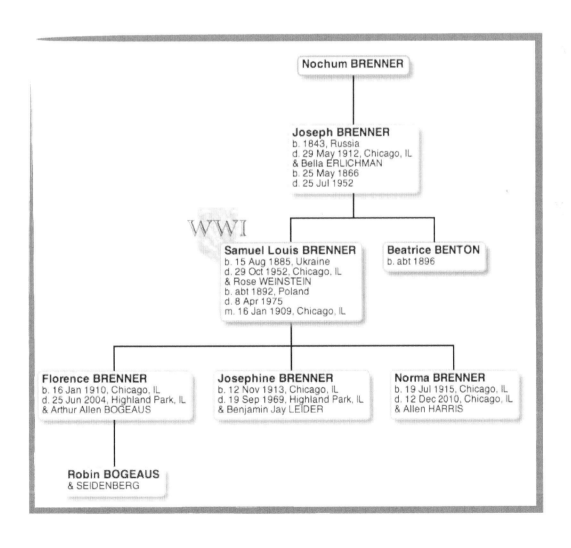

Nochum BRENNER

Joseph BRENNER
b. 1843, Russia
d. 29 May 1912, Chicago, IL
& Bella ERLICHMAN
b. 25 May 1866
d. 25 Jul 1952

WWI

Samuel Louis BRENNER
b. 15 Aug 1885, Ukraine
d. 29 Oct 1952, Chicago, IL
& Rose WEINSTEIN
b. abt 1892, Poland
d. 8 Apr 1975
m. 16 Jan 1909, Chicago, IL

Beatrice BENTON
b. abt 1896

Florence BRENNER
b. 16 Jan 1910, Chicago, IL
d. 25 Jun 2004, Highland Park, IL
& Arthur Allen BOGEAUS

Josephine BRENNER
b. 12 Nov 1913, Chicago, IL
d. 19 Sep 1969, Highland Park, IL
& Benjamin Jay LEIDER

Norma BRENNER
b. 19 Jul 1915, Chicago, IL
d. 12 Dec 2010, Chicago, IL
& Allen HARRIS

Robin BOGEAUS
& SEIDENBERG

My Grandfather Samuel L. Brenner

Robin Brenner Bogeaus Seidenberg

My maternal grandfather, Samuel L. Brenner, was a real patriot. Had he lived longer, he would have wholeheartedly concurred with the immortal words of President John F. Kennedy: "Ask not what your country can do for you — ask what you can do for your country."

I call the photo of his wife and daughters "Patriots". Grandpa tricked Bubby into signing the papers so he could fight to "save the Republic" in World War I. As the father of three children, he was exempt from military service. They would not have let him go had Bubby not signed the papers. My guess is that the "military uniform" and flags were stock props that were used for families to take photos to send to their loved ones fighting in World War I. Grandpa fought in the battles of Meuse and Argonne.

My cousins and I knew our great aunt Bea as a very elegant, very dignified lady. That was when we knew her… Through researching historical newspapers I discovered that she had had quite a theatrical career on Broadway and in Hollywood. Evidently Grandpa's patriotic service in World War I helped to inspire her career.

According to the August 12, 1924 *L.A. Times:*

"Beatrice Benton, known to thousands throughout the country as 'the Palm Olive girl', came to Southern California six months ago for a brief rest. Three years previously she had been posing for the New York artist and illustrator, Clarence F. Underwood, during which time she had become universally known as 'the girl with the schoolgirl complexion'… During the late war Miss Benton's brother [Samuel L. Brenner] was a captain overseas. She went to New York to join the Red Cross and was subsequently rejected because of her youth. Still inspired by the spirit of patriotism, the beautiful girl heard that Artist Underwood wanted a girl of her type for a patriotic government poster…Had she been accepted as a nurse it is doubtful whether the Palm Olive girl would have been created or film land blessed with another beauty."

According to family lore, Grandpa was the commanding American officer of a small town in France, and was invited to the mayor's home for dinner. Apparently meat was in short supply. He asked the mayor how they were able to serve beef. The mayor replied,

"C'est du cheval." (It is horse meat).

My grandfather, the equestrian, reportedly gagged and lost his dinner.

P.S. If you are a direct blood descendant of a World War I American veteran (father, grandfather, great grandfather…), you or your descendants could be eligible for a LaVerne Noyes scholarship. You will need to provide a copy of discharge papers or other proof of service and honorable discharge. Scholarships are available at schools as diverse as Cornell College and Cornell University. Many may have exhausted their Noyes funds, but be aware that universities now have many branches and the scholarship could be available at all the branches. Unfortunately, legally adopted children are not eligible.

http://www.senioru.com/2011/09/list-of-schools-that-offer-laverne.html lists 47 schools that offered Noyes funds as of September 17, 2001.

Charles N. Deutch

U.S. Navy

The Deutch Family in 1901 in Buffalo, NY
Left to right: Charles, Fanny, Mabel, Jacob & Lester

Deutch Family Tree

Nathan DEUTCH
b. abt 1818, Prussia/Poland
& Fradel/Frances BARON
b. abt 1827, Prussia/Poland

Jacob DEUTCH
b. abt 1860, Buffalo, NY
d. 1935, St. Louis, MO
& Fanny LOWENSTEIN
b. abt 1860, Germany
d. 1944, St. Louis, MO
m. 1884

WWI

Mabel DEUTCH
b. abt 1887, Buffalo, NY

Lester DEUTCH
b. 21 Jan 1892, Buffalo, NY
d. May 1979, St. Louis, MO

Charles N. DEUTCH
b. 24 May 1897, Buffalo, NY
d. 15 Jul 1971, San Diego, CA
& Dorothy

twin brother DEUTCH
b. 24 May 1897
d. 1897

James A. DEUTCH

My Father Charles N. Deutch

Lt. Col. (Dr.) James A. Deutch, USAF, Ret.

My father was a good man, and I loved him dearly. He was a World War I Navy veteran, and was always proud of his service to his country.

Charles Nathaniel Deutch was born on May 24, 1897. He was the third child of Jacob and Fanny Lowenstein Dutch of Buffalo, New York. He was born a twin but his brother died several months after their birth. My father's grandparents were Nathan and Fradel Baron Dutch, who came to Buffalo in November of 1851, probably from eastern Prussia.

My father was an intelligent man who had a life-long love of learning. He was forced to quit formal schooling at age 13 to help support his family, but continued his education through years of attendance at night schools. As a young teen, he went to work for Western Union Telegraph Company as a messenger boy, and over the years worked his way up to Wire Chief, retiring with 49 years of service.

My father had two stories about his life in the Navy; one humorous and the other modestly but proudly told. My dad was a healthy young man, but not a man of muscle and brawn. He did his "boot camp" at what is now called Naval Station Great Lakes, near Chicago, Illinois. In order to get the recruits into shape, the Navy provided a very large hill of coal with a ramp running up, across, and down the other side. The objective was to move the hill of coal from point A to point B. Each recruit would run a coal laden wheelbarrow up, across, and down the hill of coal, and then on to point B. My father told me about the several times his wheel barrel got dumped, until he got into shape. How many times the hill of coal was moved from point A to Point B, and back again, he never did say.

Because of his superior ability to read, copy and send Morse Code, after boot camp, my father, was assigned to the staff of Secretary of the Navy, Josephus Daniels, at the War Department, in Washington, D.C. For those who do not know, Morse Code, as used in the War Department, was a method of transmitting text as a series of clicks that could be directly understood by a skilled listener. In November 1918, Seaman Charles N. Deutch was assigned to decode and copy the original version of the *Treaty of Versailles*. My dad always referred to this document as "The German Peace Treaty." My father, a professional telegrapher, thought this was the most important contribution of his military career.

Following the war, Secretary of the Navy Daniels personally asked my father to remain on his staff. As were many young men, my father was eager to return home and resume his life as a civilian. Years later, my father told me that perhaps he should have remained in the Navy, and urged me to think about a military career for myself. I did so, and in my father's footsteps proudly served my country as an Air Force officer for 23 years.

Of genealogical interest is the fact that my father's mother, Fanny Lowenstein Deutch (b. 1860), was the 20th child of Hayum and Rosgen Fuld Lowenstein of Langendernbach, Germany. Nineteen of the 20 children lived and had children of their own. Fanny's older sister, Lena Lowenstein (b. 1852) married my grandfather's older brother Aaron (b 1855), and is my great aunt.

My grandfather, Jacob, changed the family name from Dutch to Deutch after the U.S. Federal Census of 1900 and before the next census in 1910.

Charles, age 72, and his newly awarded high school diploma

Eichwald Family

Matt & his mother Celia

Cousin Matt served
in the American
Expeditionary
Force

Wilhelm

Wilhelm & Julius,
German soldiers
in France

Eichwald Family Tree

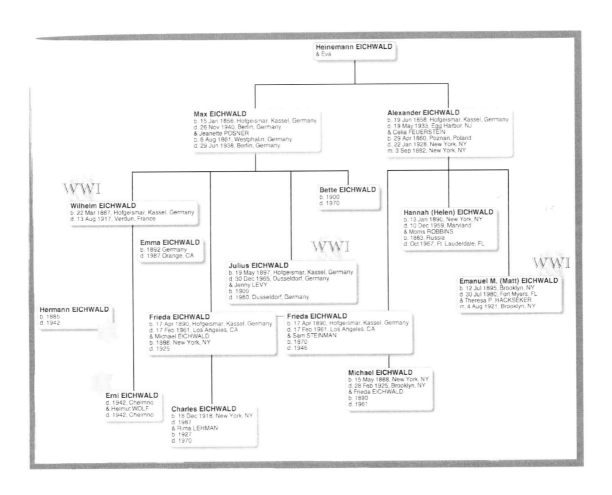

Wilhelm and Julius Eichwald

Jeanette Shelburne

My great uncles, Wilhelm and Julius Eichwald were among the patriotic German Jews who enthusiastically volunteered to fight for the Fatherland when World War I began in 1914. Wilhelm was 27 and Julius was only 16. At that time, the Eichwald family was proudly assimilated into German society while still preserving their Jewish identity and practices.

Wilhelm and Julius' father, Max Eichwald was the owner of a successful shoe and dry goods business in Kassel, a lovely traditional town nestled in one of those quintessential beautiful German landscapes of forests, streams and bright green rolling hills dotted with hilltop castles in central Germany. There, the family lived an elegant and cultured lifestyle. Their sister, Frieda (my grandmother) remembered how, before the start of World War I, she enjoyed dancing with the military officers who were stationed nearby. During World War I, Max converted his business to manufacture boots for the army.

Many German Jewish men were similarly enthusiastic to serve the Fatherland. At that time, middle-class German Jews prospered and a few grew rich. Grand synagogues rose in the main cities and Jewish citizens became avid supporters of the arts. Many excelled in commerce and science. There was still a gulf separating Jews from the apex of German power so some young men hoped that by volunteering before they were called up, it would help overcome the informal barriers to full integration in German society. Many joined to defeat Russia, shocked by the continuing brutal Russian pogroms. Intoxicated by pride in their German culture, the young soldiers expected a quick and easy victory.

By 1915 the Western Front had become a stalemate as both sides engaged in trench warfare. Unable to achieve a decisive breakthrough, offensives simply resulted in heavy casualties with little gain. Seeking to shatter the Anglo-French lines, the German Chief of Staff, Erich von Falkenhayn, planned a massive assault on the French city of Verdun. Wilhelm fought in this battle, the longest and most demanding battle of World War I, which began in February of 1916.

From the beginning the casualties mounted quickly on both sides and after some early gains of territory by the Germans, the battle settled into a bloody stalemate of trench warfare. On December 18, 1917, Hindenberg finally called a stop to the German attacks after 10 long months. With a German death toll of 143,000 (out of 377,000 total casualties) and a French one of 162,440 (out of 37,231 total casualties), Verdun would come to signify, more than any other battle, the grinding, bloody nature of warfare on the Western Front during World War I.

Wilhelm Eichwald was killed at Verdun on August 13, 1917. He is buried there in an unmarked grave. Julius Eichwald fared better. He survived the war and was highly decorated for bravery. After the war he became a famous shoe designer and travelled to the major capitals of Europe where large manufacturers desired his designs.   When the Nazis came to power Julius was able to avoid persecution for a time because he made sure to always wear the pin of his regiment, one that was well respected for its valor in World War I. Thus, he was able to arrange emigration from Germany in December of 1938, just 9 months before the Second World War broke out, and travel to America where his sisters, Frieda and Bette were living. (Frieda had emigrated in 1913 in order to marry her cousin, Michael Eichwald and Bette came in 1926 to help Frieda after Michael passed away.)

In spite of the Eichwald brothers' patriotism and sacrifice for their country, the rest of their family left in Germany was destroyed by the Nazi regime.

Wilhelm's daughter, Erni and her husband, Helmut Wolff and one-year-old daughter Tana, were deported from Berlin in 1941 to the Lodz ghetto and then to Chelmno concentration camp where they were murdered in 1942. Their brother, Hermann was also murdered by the Nazis. Their sister, Emma was protected by her non-Jewish husband Fritz Fenker for most of the war although his refusal to divorce and repudiate her cost him his successful career as an architect. Unfortunately, Fritz died in 1944, leaving Emma without protection as the spouse of a non-Jew. Since she was already undergoing surgery to correct a weakness in her eyes, Emma bribed the surgeons to keep her in the hospital as a patient; otherwise she faced deportation and probable death. One by one, she kept giving them pieces of her jewelry to perform unnecessary operations; and by the time the war was over, she had survived but was blind. She was able to immigrate to the US within a few years to live with her sister, my grandmother Frieda in California. Blessedly, their parents, Max and Jeanette died natural deaths before 1940 in Berlin.

After the end of World War II, Julius married Jenny Levy (also German-born) in the USA and eventually, they returned to Germany. He was one of the many German Jews who never felt at home in their adopted countries and so returned to live in the land they had once loved, in spite of what had been done to their families and fellow Jews by the Nazis. It must have been a painful decision and adjustment for Julius and his wife. He attempted to get reparations, but was unsuccessful due to bureaucratic stalemates. Julius lived in Dusseldorf with these haunting memories until he passed away in 1965. Jenny remained there until she died in 1980.

When I was growing up, I loved spending time with my aunt Emma, a sweet, blind elderly lady who always had a beloved cat. Once I was surprised to hear her say, "Germany is the most wonderful country in the world." "How can you say that after what they did to you?" I asked. She replied, "That was the Nazis, that isn't Germany. Before the Nazis took over, we had a wonderful life." Then she hummed to herself, reliving her beautiful memories, behind her big dark glasses.

Matthew Eichwald

Robert Wagner

While I never heard first hand if any of my maternal great uncles served during the Great War, I came across a letter from 1919 addressed to my grandmother, written by her brother Emanuel M. "Matt" Eichwald while he served in the American Expeditionary Forces (AEF) at age 23. While we don't know if he saw action in Europe during the war, the letter he wrote was dated four months after the Treaty of Versailles formally ending the war. The only clue as to his location was a brief reference to "getting along well with the Germans." Fortunately, my grandmother Hannah "Helen" Eichwald Robbins kept an album of photographs and letters among which I also discovered a postcard written by Matt to his mother Celia that he penned while sailing on the cruiser *USS Seattle* in May, but the year was not legible. All he said was "Dear Mother, Back again. Will try and see you soon." On the lower left, though, was a key piece of information that confirmed he was part of the Occupation Forces in Germany after the war. His military unit was filled in as "Batt E, Reg 324, Div 32nd" which upon further research I found that the 32nd Division of the AEF were stationed in Germany during the Occupation. He was returning to New York aboard a commonly used troop transport ship that ferried soldiers from Brest, France to New York, even during the war. Records show that the *USS Seattle* embarked on May 10, 1919 with soldiers of the 324th.

Searching for more information about his unit revealed that there was a complete book online about the history of the 324th Field Artillery (324 F.A.), a unit of the 32nd Division AEF. More remarkably, towards the end was a complete roster of all those who served with the 324th F.A., formed in 1917 when the U.S. entered the war. Under the heading of "Battery E", I found my Great Uncle listed with the same address in Brooklyn as his parents. Uncle Matt, born in 1895, came from a large family of 10 siblings including six brothers, and at least two other brothers filed Draft Registration cards as was required of most young men. Both his parents immigrated from Germany in 1870s, and his father Alexander Eichwald had a brother Max who lived in Kassel, Germany. Two of Max's sons, Wilhelm and Julius Eichwald who were first cousins to Matt, served in the German Army. By the time that Uncle Matt served with the AEF, his cousin Wilhelm had been killed in the Battle of Verdun in 1917 and was never found. Julius survived the war and served with distinction in an elite unit. After the war, Julius came to the U.S. in 1937 to escape the persecution that lead up to the Second World War.

EICHWALD, EMANUEL MATTHEW
(Last Name)   (Other Names)

1485 Gaylord Terr., W. Englewood, N.J.
(Address)

SA-Spanish	AQ-Aqueduct
MX-Mex. Bdr.	CS-Consp. Serv.
WW-World War	R-Recruiting

MEDAL	NO.	DATE ISSUED	ORGANIZATION SERVED WITH
WW	48162	11/5/37	Cpl. Bat. E. 324 H.F.A.

award of medal other than Decoration for Long
and Faithful Service.
500 (1B-8809)

AMERICAN
YMCA

ON ACTIVE SERVICE
WITH THE
AMERICAN EXPEDITIONARY FORCE

Mar. 16   1919

Dear Sister Helen:

Inclose you will find a souvenir from France. Which I hope you will like. Also I received all the papers you have sent me ok.

Was very glad to get them. How is everything getting along? We are having a fine time here, and get along very well with the Germans.

Well I will close hoping you are all ok And best wishes to you & all home.

Remains
Your brother
Matt.

Emanuel
Matthew
Eichwald

POST CARD

Correspondence

Dear Mother:
Back again. Will try
and see you soon.

Arrived on U.S. Seattle
Going to Camp Merritt

Signature Matt.

Bat. E. Reg 324 Div 32

This Side for Address

Mrs. C. Eichwald
1150 Flatbush Ave
Brooklyn
New York

U.S.S.
SOLDIERS
MAIL
SEATTLE

33

Chaim Finkelstein

Canada, Ocean Arrivals (Form 30A), 1919-1924

Chaim was a Russian soldier from Slutsk, Belarus who went AWOL. He then managed to get to Bucharest, where he arranged passage to Canada. He sailed on the vessel *Braga* 7 September 1924 and was headed to Montréal with the support of the Jewish Colonization Association. His family later heard from him in a letter sent from Winnipeg, Manitoba, Canada.

Chaim Finkelstein

Paul Pascal

My maternal grandparents, Avrom-Ahron Micheikin and Tsipa Finkelstein Micheikin, came from the town of Slutsk and the area around it—now in Belarus but which was in Czarist Russia at the time of this story. My grandmother's brother, Chaim Finkelstein, was among several young Jewish men of draft age who were being conscripted into the Czar's army at the beginning of the First World War. Chaim's conscription came not long after his arranged marriage to a young woman who shall remain nameless in this story—she would not have been Chaim's first choice for a wife.

 The young Jews who were heading off to war were the occasion for a Jewish legal problem (not only in Slutsk but throughout the Jewish world). If, God forbid, one of them was killed in battle but his body not recovered, there would be no proof that his wife was actually a widow. She would not be able to re-marry, because there was, legally speaking, the *possibility* that she was still married to a living man. The problem was a technicality of law, but binding nonetheless, so the rabbis in their resourcefulness came up with a solution that was also a technicality of law. The wife of each draftee in Slutsk was issued a *tnai-get*—a conditional divorce document. When a husband returned from the war, his wife could happily tear up the paper. But if a husband did not return from war, she would not have to prove that he was dead; she could present this document, which would render the couple legally divorced, and she would be able to remarry.

The wives of Chaim and of his cousin, my great-uncle Sender Finkelstein, were each issued a *tnai-get.* When Sender was told of it, he broke down crying. When Chaim was told of it, he jumped for joy. As it turned out, Sender returned from the war in one piece. But by the end of the war, Chaim had not returned. My grandmother was beside herself with grief over her little brother. "What has become of my Chaim'l's bones?" she wailed in Yiddish.

If my grandmother had at that moment become aware of where her little brother's bones were, she would likely have wrung his neck: Chaim had gone AWOL and was very much alive—the *tnai-get* had set him free.

The family did not hear from Chaim until seven years later, when he sent them a letter from Winnipeg, Canada. We are still not sure of all of his wanderings during that long period of silence, except for proof we found that showed he crossed the Atlantic from a port in Romania, under the sponsorship of Baron De Hirsch's Jewish Colonization Association. On his passport, he claimed to have been born in Starokonstantinov, Ukraine. Perhaps Chaim believed that this lie was necessary to help him evade the possibility of arrest for desertion. He needn't have worried, though; the czarist regime that had sent him off to war was no more, replaced by the Bolsheviks and their USSR, through a revolution that was in part triggered by the thousands of Russian soldiers who went AWOL during World War I.

Arthur Frank

German Army serving in France

Arthur is standing, second from the right

Frank
Family Tree

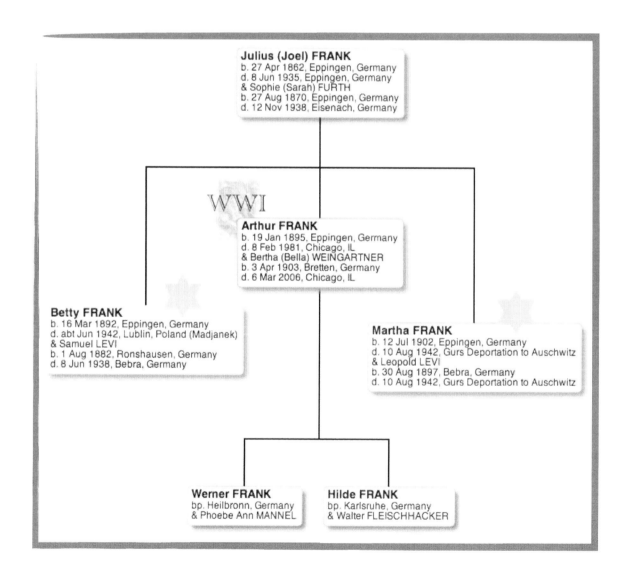

Julius (Joel) FRANK
b. 27 Apr 1862, Eppingen, Germany
d. 8 Jun 1935, Eppingen, Germany
& Sophie (Sarah) FURTH
b. 27 Aug 1870, Eppingen, Germany
d. 12 Nov 1938, Eisenach, Germany

WWI

Arthur FRANK
b. 19 Jan 1895, Eppingen, Germany
d. 8 Feb 1981, Chicago, IL
& Bertha (Bella) WEINGARTNER
b. 3 Apr 1903, Bretten, Germany
d. 6 Mar 2006, Chicago, IL

Betty FRANK
b. 16 Mar 1892, Eppingen, Germany
d. abt Jun 1942, Lublin, Poland (Madjanek)
& Samuel LEVI
b. 1 Aug 1882, Ronshausen, Germany
d. 8 Jun 1938, Bebra, Germany

Martha FRANK
b. 12 Jul 1902, Eppingen, Germany
d. 10 Aug 1942, Gurs Deportation to Auschwitz
& Leopold LEVI
b. 30 Aug 1897, Bebra, Germany
d. 10 Aug 1942, Gurs Deportation to Auschwitz

Werner FRANK
bp. Heilbronn, Germany
& Phoebe Ann MANNEL

Hilde FRANK
bp. Karlsruhe, Germany
& Walter FLEISCHHACKER

My Father's Three Lives

Werner L. Frank

I grew up with the story that my father was born twice. This tale always amazed me and led to the often repeated story of how his birth was celebrated two times, once in 1895 and the second in 1918, twenty-three years later. I recall being told that a communiqué from the German military pronounced my father killed-in-action on a battlefield in France during World War I. Subsequently, his parents were informed that he was actually alive but severely wounded. He came home to recuperate and the family welcomed him back with a second birth party.

My childhood curiosity caused me to further explore what happened to my father during the war, what battle took place and how he was wounded. In response, I recall my father pointing to the front, left side of his neck which showed a slight scar, and then tracing with his hand a trajectory to the back of his upper torso. He simply said, "The bullet went through my lungs and came out the back." On one such occasion he actually removed his undershirt and showed me the exit scar on his back. I asked him if he had had any lingering side effects, to which he replied that he had none.

That was as far as I ever took the matter. I had concluded that since he was serving in the German army in France as a *Frontsoldat* (soldier at the frontline of battle), he must have been shot by some Frenchman. My level of interest at the time was satisfied; I failed to elicit more details and facts about this milestone event.

Years later, after undertaking serious research of my family's history and genealogy, I was disappointed that I had not probed further regarding my father's wartime experience. It was too late to address needed questions to my father. He passed away in 1981. How could I now piece together a significant history that had eluded me?

The pages of former issues of *Stammbaum* were one source of information on the subject of Jewish participation in the armies fielded by Germany. Claus K. Hirsch has delved into this matter in two articles, one related to the Prussian wars of 1813-1815[1] and the second describing Jewish soldiers' participation in World War I.[2] Other articles have appeared as well.[3] Bibliographies accompany these articles and provide further insight to the loyalty and service given by Jewish young men to their Fatherland. However, this type of information does not get down to the specifics of the individual's life and his performance in the military.[4] I wanted to know specifically what my father had sacrificed and given to his country.

Luck was with me. In a collection of family memorabilia, my father had actually retained his *Militärpaß*, a personal identification booklet containing his service record, as well as a number of service related photographs. The journal accounted for my father's front-line duty in the form of a soldier's personal diary. It also contained vital information regarding his induction, training, promotions, awards and duties. Fortunately, this extraordinary notebook and the accompanying photos survived our family's upheaval and immigration to the U.S.A. in 1937 and are still in my possession.

My father was *Vizewachtmeister* (Master Sergeant) Arthur Frank, a volunteer (*Kriegsfreiwilliger*) who joined the Kaiser's army on 30 December 1914, one month before his 20th birthday. He was initially assigned to the II Ersatz-Abteilung, 5th Baden Field Artillery, 76th Regiment, with headquarters at Freiburg. On 25 April 1915 he was transferred to the 6th Battery of the 76th Regiment and remained there until the end of the war.

A noteworthy member of the 76th Regiment was an officer who became a notorious underground "freedom" fighter after the war. This was Albert Leo Schlageter, a comrade-in-arms of my father. Schlageter terrorized the

French occupation of the Ruhr in the early 1920s. He was ultimately captured after detonating a bridge near Calcum in March 1923. Subsequently, he was tried by the French, found guilty of sabotage, and faced a firing squad. He died in May 1923, becoming a national martyr, revered by the Nazis, whom he had actually joined in 1922, carrying the early membership number 61.

Some of Schlageter's notoriety rubbed off on my father. Accordingly, there were gentiles in my father's hometown of Eppingen who doubted that the reach of the Nazis could ever extend to a Jew who was a field comrade of Schlageter. Little did they realize that no Jew could escape the wrath and hate of the Nazis.

Skirmishes and battles for my father's unit began in the period 9-10 August 1914 at Senheim-Mülhausen, extending over the next four years to Lothringen, Nancy-Epinal, Flirey, Arras, Lille, French Flanders, Cuinchy, Auchy-lez-La Bassée, Champagne, Somme, Bapaume, Scarpe, etc. It is not clear if my father was involved in all of these encounters. However, we do know with certainty that he fought in the battle at Bapaume from 21 August to 2 September 1918 and at the Siegfried line from 3 to 27 September 1918.

On 27 September, at 12:30 p.m., in a firing position 1 kilometer east of Bourlon, my father received a severe neck and chest injury. A bullet found its mark, entering the front of my father's throat and passed through his lungs before exiting from his back. He fell to the ground at a moment when the Allied forces were advancing to take control of the battlefield. The retreating German forces left my father for dead. According to family lore, his body lay immobile, seemingly without breath, and his fellow comrades assumed he was dead.

Somewhat later, the German forces went on the offensive and recaptured the territory. A soldier stumbled over my father's body and discovered that he was still alive. The medics immediately tended to him and he was revived. He was then transferred to Field Hospital number 24 and, on 4 October 1918, was transported by hospital train number 28 to St. Anna Lyceum Hospital in Elberfeld, where he recovered.

With such detailed information, I next wanted to pursue collateral records of my father by contacting appropriate contemporary German authorities that might be able to shed further light on his military service. The logical place of contact was the *Bundesarchiv* (the National Archive of Germany) at www.bundesarchiv.de . Here I discovered that there were several archival components, one of which was the Military Archive located in Freiburg and having its own website at www.bundesarchiv.de/aufgaben_organisation/ abteilungen/ma/index.html . Upon addressing my interest by email (militaerarchiv@barch.bund.de), I received a prompt reply indicating to their sorrow that all records of individual soldiers of World War I were destroyed by Allied bombing of the *Heeresarchiv* in Potsdam in 1945. What was I to do now? I turned to the Internet.

I had always assumed that my father had been a casualty of the French forces. My understanding of the circumstances of his field injury on that crucial September date in 1918 was substantially clarified when I investigated relevant websites on the World Wide Web while I was researching the completion of a book on the history of my family.[5] I was astounded to find so much detail regarding the progression of World War I battles, their location and time. Simply entering "Bourlon 1918" into the *Google* search engine provided me with rich details concerning the very events of the time and place my father had been shot.

The wonders of the Internet for contemporary researchers became apparent. One website suggested that it was Canadian troops who were responsible for my father's injuries by offering the following account:[6]

It was found that the Bosche had taken up a defensive line on the eastern side of the Canal du Nord and so we were compelled to establish our line on the western bank, as all bridges over the canal had been destroyed . . . On the night of the 25th [September, 1918] a move forward was made to the concentration area around Bullocourt, where the Battalion was scattered over the old battlefield in shell holes, dugouts, etc. The Battalion moved forward to their assembly area in the old Hindenburg line just west of Inchy en Artois . . . .

The 11th Brigade had been given the task of capturing Bourlon Wood after the 10th Brigade had got across the canal, and at zero hour, 5:20 A.M. on the 27th of September, commenced to move forward, the 102nd Battalion leading, followed by the 87th, 54th and 75th Battalions.The task of this Battalion [the 54th] was to get around the north side of Bourlon Wood and capture the northern and eastern portion of the wood . . . . Bourlon Wood was on high commanding ground and it was vital that this ground should be in our hands before the 3rd Army commenced their attack. Accordingly it was arranged that the 54th Battalion, on capturing the eastern side of the wood, was to send up a star rocket to signify that this high ground was taken.

The Canal du Nord was crossed without casualties and the Battalion jumped off without delay, and after stiff fighting managed to establish themselves on the eastern side of the wood, sending up the signal that the wood was captured.

By other accounts, 27 September 1918 was a pivotal day that turned the tide of the war in favor of the Allies who broke through the Hindenburg (a.k.a. Siegfried) Line and subsequently took Cambrai.[7] These battles precipitated the end of the war on 11 November 1918.

My father's apparent fate caused a needless shock to his family. Immediately after the regiment's retreat from the battlefield where my father had been shot, his well-meaning battery commander, in his zeal to inform families of battlefield victims, wrote the following letter of condolence to my grandfather (translated from the original German):

In the battlefield, Sept. 29, 1918

Dear Mr. Frank.
[addressed to Julius Frank, father of Arthur Frank]

As the current Battery Commander of the 6th Field Battery, 76th Regiment, I must, with deepest sadness, inform you of the news that your dear son Arthur died a hero's death for the Fatherland on Sep 27. A shot in the neck was the cause of death. Unfortunately, it was not possible to retrieve his mortal remains, and so Arthur lies buried in the same town in which his early death came about.

Since his time in the Battery, Arthur and I have been close friends, and he was a likable, good comrade with whom I shared both sorrow and joy. His commanders all were satisfied with his performance as was I, which should be clear from the fact that he had been recommended for the *E.K. I Klasse*[8] and would have become an officer on the next occasion. I discussed both of these matters with him two days before his death, so at least he was still able to enjoy these prospects. Unfortunately, fate would have it that he would not live to achieve either.

Arthur was a model, capable, conscientious and energetic *Vizewachmeister*. To me he was not only a well-thought-of comrade, but he also was a dear and trustworthy friend. I had the good fortune to have been together with him since May 15, except for short breaks, during which time I learned to like and respect him.

Arthur Frank will forever be remembered by myself and the entire Battery, honoring his memory.

Since I share the great sorrow with the caring father, the beloved mother, and the rest of the family, I send you my deepest sympathy.

Yours,
(Signed) Eberle
Art. F. R. *und Batterieführer*

My family in Eppingen was devastated by this news, grieving in deep sorrow. What terrible pain Julius and his wife Sophie Frank must have felt, realizing that the war was rapidly coming to an end and their son was never to return home again. Fortunately, they were soon informed of the grave error and that Arthur, my father, was recovering in a field hospital.

The Frank family held a happy "second birth" party upon the return of their son to Eppingen.

The loyalty to Germany shown by young Jewish men on the battlefields of World War I did not grant them any special consideration from the Nazis some fifteen years later. At first, as the Nazis undertook their mounting program of hate against Jews, it was thought that those who had served and shed their blood for the Fatherland would be respected. Indeed, some were actually singled out for so-called special handling by being sent to the concentration camp at Theresienstadt.[9] In the end, of course, all Jews were given equal treatment with respect to the "final solution." No matter what their contribution to German society may have been, Jews were despised, disenfranchised and ultimately destined to the death camps.

Fortunately, my father had the wisdom to save our family by our relatively early immigration to the U.S.A. in 1937. Perhaps this warrants my father with yet another re-birth, the miracle of survival from the tyranny of the Holocaust and the gift of a third life.

[1] Hirsch, Claus W., "Jewish Soldiers in the Prussian Liberation Wars, 1813-1815", *Stammbaum*, Issue 3, Summer 1993.

[2] Hirsch, Claus W., "German-Jewish Soldiers in World War I", *Stammbaum*, Issue 10, December 1996.

[3] Mautner, Herb, "Jewish Members of the German Airforce during WWI", *Stammbaum*, Issue 11, June 1997.
  Davidson Baird, Carol, "World War I German Cemeteries in France", *Stammbaum*, Issue 14, December 1998.
  Schmidl, Erwin A., "Jewish Soldiers in the Austrian Armed Forces", *Stammbaum*, Issue 19, Summer 2001.

[4] An exception is the book <u>Gefallene Deutsche Juden, Frontbriefe</u> 1914-1918 [Fallen Jewish Soldiers, Letters from the Front, 1914-1918], published by Reichsbund Jüdischer Frontsoldaten, Vortrupp Verlag, Berlin, second edition 1935. Here at least one is able to discern the individual feelings of the soldier at the front.

[5] Frank, Werner L., *Legacy: The Saga of a German-Jewish Family Across Time and Circumstance*, Avotaynu Foundation Inc., Bergenfield, N.J., 2003.

[6] Diary of the 54th Battalion, Canadian forces of the 3rd Army, at the website: http://members.tripod.com/apollon_2/warpages/ops1918_3htm

[7] The detailed Order of Battle of the Canadian forces at Bourlon is described in the series *For King & Empire, Volume 6: The Canadians at Cambrai and the Canal du Nord, September-October 1918*, authored by Norm M. Christie and published by CEF Books of Ottawa, Canada, in 1997.

[8] Iron Cross, First Class.

[9] Theresienstadt was supposedly a unique concentration camp, established by the Nazis to incarcerate, among others, noted Jews and war veterans. In truth, it was more of a holding pen for captives who were ultimately transported to the death camps.

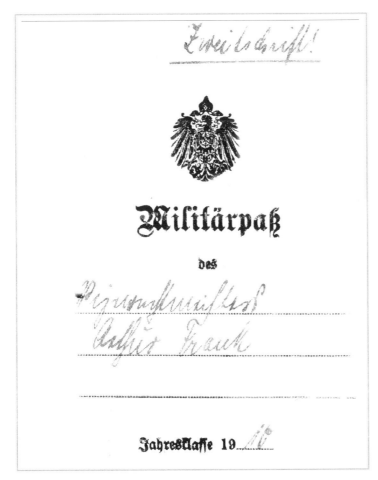

A page from the military diary of Arthur Frank and his military pass

Roman
Freulich

The Jewish Legion

Freulich
Family Tree

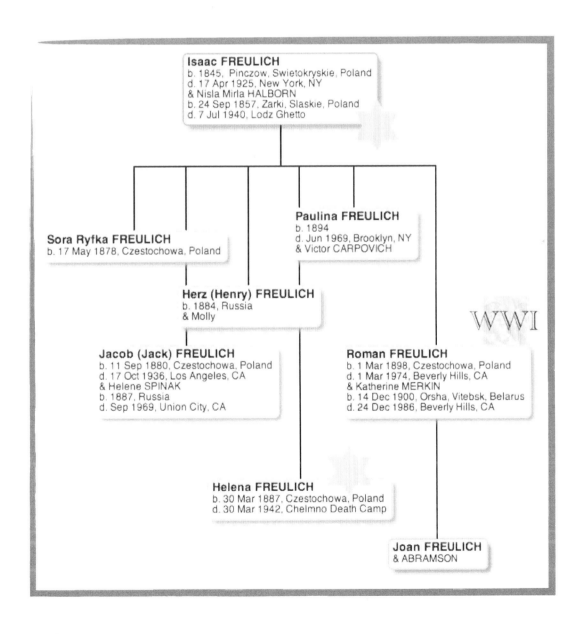

Isaac FREULICH
b. 1845, Pinczow, Swietokryskie, Poland
d. 17 Apr 1925, New York, NY
& Nisla Mirla HALBORN
b. 24 Sep 1857, Zarki, Slaskie, Poland
d. 7 Jul 1940, Lodz Ghetto

Paulina FREULICH
b. 1894
d. Jun 1969, Brooklyn, NY
& Victor CARPOVICH

Sora Ryfka FREULICH
b. 17 May 1878, Czestochowa, Poland

Herz (Henry) FREULICH
b. 1884, Russia
& Molly

Jacob (Jack) FREULICH
b. 11 Sep 1880, Czestochowa, Poland
d. 17 Oct 1936, Los Angeles, CA
& Helene SPINAK
b. 1887, Russia
d. Sep 1969, Union City, CA

Roman FREULICH
b. 1 Mar 1898, Czestochowa, Poland
d. 1 Mar 1974, Beverly Hills, CA
& Katherine MERKIN
b. 14 Dec 1900, Orsha, Vitebsk, Belarus
d. 24 Dec 1986, Beverly Hills, CA

WWI

Helena FREULICH
b. 30 Mar 1887, Czestochowa, Poland
d. 30 Mar 1942, Chelmno Death Camp

Joan FREULICH
& ABRAMSON

The Jewish Legion

Joan Abramson

During the first years of World War I, a debate began among young Jewish immigrant men living in America: should they, or shouldn't they, enlist to fight on the side of the Allies?

In 1914 the British Army organized several battalions of the Royal Fusiliers as exclusively Jewish units. The first unit came to be known as the Zion Mule Corps and took an active role in the British campaign in Gallipoli. Later units were known as the Jewish Legion and fought in Egypt, Syria and Palestine.

Recruitment in Canada and the United States was active, but there were many Jewish immigrants who did not rush to join the British brigades. Many had arrived in the United States, as had Roman Freulich, in flight from possible conscription into the czarist army and in hope of escaping the oppressive czarist regime. Why would they now turn around and fight on the side of that same czarist regime?

Two 1917 events changed the debate. One was the signing of the Balfour Declaration, proclaiming British support for a national home for the Jewish people in Palestine. The second was the beginning of the Russian Revolution. With that revolution, Russia's role as an active Allied partner faded. Once Czarist Russia was no longer a factor young Jewish immigrants in America began to cross the border into Canada in order to join the British Royal Fusiliers: the Jewish Legion.

in all, about 10,000 young Jews from all over the world enlisted in the Legion. They served primarily in Egypt and Palestine, fighting against Ottoman troops. Following the Armistice of November 11, 1918, they remained in the British Mandate of Palestine and took part in the defense of Jewish communities faced with Arab riots. My father, Roman Freulich, was part of that effort.

Years later, Freulich wrote an anecdotal account of life among the Jewish Legionnaires, titled *Soldiers in Judea*. His collection of photographs from his Legion days is currently housed in the Skirball Museum and the Simon Wiesenthal Center, both in Los Angeles, California and Beit Hagdudim in Avichail, Israel.

The short introduction to the Jewish Legion, above, and the photographs on the next page, are part of a family history I just completed with a cousin who lives in Warsaw. The book, called *The Halborns: Ancestors Immigrants Survivors*, was published in Warsaw. My father, Roman Freulich, was the son of Nisla Halborn Freulich, who was a Shoah victim, killed in the Lodz ghetto.

After World War One, Freulich moved to Los Angeles and became a well known Hollywood photographer.

The two photographs on the next page are among the many Freulich took during his service with the Jewish Legion. One depicts a Legionnaire guarding the graves of comrades who lost their lives while serving in the Legion. A second shows a group of Legionnaires on a visit to the pyramids while serving in Egypt. A number of other photographs were taken by Freulich during his service. During later reunions his comrades often commented that he was always taking pictures and that he was often found using sun printing, a process using a UV light source to develop negatives.

George Gal

In the Streets of Budapest

Andrew Gal

My father, George Gal was born in 1909 and lived in Budapest.

He tells me the story that the Hungarian troops who were going to the front held a parade through the streets of Budapest. The population was very excited and everyone was saying "long live the glorious war."

As a 6 year old he went to watch, and climbed a lamp post to get a good view. He, like all Hungarian Jews, was an extremely patriotic Hungarian and very proud to see the soldiers.

Suddenly, the soldiers started singing an anti-semitic song. He told me, that he felt as if someone threw a bucket of cold water over him. He immediately climbed off the lamp post and slunk home.

Worse was to come a few decades later.

Jack Goldenberg

British in Egypt

Myra Waddell

Lancashire Fusiliers and
38th Royal Fusiliers

Jack Goldenberg, son of
Hyman & Leah Goldenberg
of Liverpool, England was killed
17 December 1918 in Egypt.

He was born in
Paris, France in 1898.
His parents were born
in Bucharest, Romania.

He is buried in the
Kantara War Memorial
Cemetery, located on the
eastern side of the Suez Canal,
about 130 km NE of Cairo.

*Commonwealth War Graves
Commission
& British Census Records*

Leopold
(Lipot)
Goldstein

Rabbi, or not?

Leopold and his wife Gizella, and daughter Roze
in Kezmarok, Slovakia

Leopold Goldstein

Madeleine Isenberg

Of the families I have researched, the only person who seemingly played a significant role in the first world war was my paternal grandfather Leopold/Lipot "Aryeh" Goldstein. He was born 11 August 1882 in what is now Szina, just south of Slovakia's second largest city, Kosice. Leopold must have demonstrated excellent scholarship especially in Judaic studies. Because when he was about 18 he traveled eastward, some 450 km away to the even larger city of Pressburg (now Bratislava), to attend the prestigious *yeshiva*[1] of the highly respected Chatam-Sofer. In addition to his given knowledge of Hebrew and Yiddish, archived school records indicate he was there until 1903 and that he spoke both German and Hungarian, also considered valuable assets in the army. While I have no written proof, I presume he finished studies, gained ordination in 1903, and then joined the Royal Hungarian Army. All 21-year old men were compelled to join, but by then, army service had been reduced from seven to three years. Presumably due to his ordination Leopold became a reserve *Feldrabbiner* (field-rabbi/chaplain).

In the beautiful Tatra Mountains region of Slovakia lived the Goldman family with an eligible daughter, Gizella. Father Isak wanted to find a suitable, well-educated *shidduch*[2] for his eldest daughter and consulted with the local chief rabbi, Rabbi Abraham Grünburg. I believe this rabbi must have turned to his son,

Rabbi Simcha Nathan Grünburg, of similar marriageable age. I deduced he had been a friend of the very learned Leopold Goldstein at the same *yeshiva* and hence recommended him. Rabbi Abraham Grünburg officiated at their marriage on 5th March 1907 in Kezmarok and they settled there.

The Goldman family was reasonably comfortable, dealing with all aspects related to cattle: cheese-manufacturing, butcher shops, cattle brokering, and tanning of hides. According to family stories, father-in-law Isak Goldman set Leopold up in the foul-smelling, skin-discoloring, hide-tanning process. It wasn't meant to be demeaning, but the other businesses were all well-covered by family members long before he arrived. But this was not exactly what my grandfather had envisioned for his future life. He was more of a "*luftmensch*," more interested in airy intellectual pursuits than practical matters like earning an income. He would have preferred to spend time with his scholarly books and assisting the Rabbi in addressing religious life issues in their Jewish community.

In time children were born: Roze "Rachel" (Feb 1908), Jindrich "Chaim," (my father, in July 1909), and Arpad "Avraham Yakov" (May 1911).

With three children in tow, suddenly they upped and moved 550 km southward to Timisoara, Romania. Maybe he wanted to run away from that distasteful, smelly job. Unsubstantiated lore says that he and Gizella opened a bed-and-breakfast for Orthodox Jewish vacationers in what was then a large resort town. We know he was there pre-World War I because yet another child, Helen "Hinde" was born there in June 1913.

With the outbreak of World War I, a month after Archduke Franz-Ferdinand's assassination (24 June 1914), and Gizella again pregnant, they must have decided to return to Kezmarok, because Leopold would doubtless be called up in his reserve chaplain's capacity, and who would care for the family? Birth record show that daughter, Blanca "Beila" arrived (February 1915) in Kezmarok. I assume he was home a lot because another son, Izidor "Sruli" arrived (March 1917).

Documentation exists (in Hungarian) regarding personnel in the Royal Hungarian Army and grandfather's name is listed with the reserve rabbis for years 1915-1918 (see page 60). No photos of him exist between 1910–1934, so I don't know what red-headed and -bearded, blue-eyed Leopold might have looked like in uniform, but learned that chaplain's coats had three stripes on their sleeves (chaplains bore the rank of captain). These chaplains had specific functions when catering to Jewish soldiers, especially in providing kosher food!

Historically, World War I ended at 11:00 AM, November 11, 1918. Around that date certain events must have been shock-provoking to my great-grandparents, Leopold's parents, in their Kosice milieu. On November 10, their Kaiser, Charles I of Austria-Hungary abdicated. The following day, Germany signed the Armistice of Compiègne at 6:00 AM and five hours later, fighting actually ended. On November 12, Austria was proclaimed a Republic, and two days later, the Republic of Czechoslovakia came into being. Only four days later (November 18, 1918), Leopold's father, my great-grandfather Joseph Goldstein, died in a brand-new country without ever having left home.

Over time, I've been unable to completely certify with written proof that grandfather was indeed a rabbi. But I do know that his scholarship and acumen were well appreciated. To demonstrate, a descendent of the Grünburg rabbis sent me a copy of a handwritten, Judeo-German[3] testimony (dated 1923) from the town's *Beth Din* (Jewish Court of Law). It's for an *agunah*[4] widow, who could not prove that her husband (Osias/Yehoshua Weiser) had died: Two Jewish soldiers (Yisrael Goldman and Josef Gerhardt) attested that her husband had died in October 1916, and that he was buried in a non-Jewish cemetery. Three judges' names appear at the bottom of the testimony: Chief Rabbi Simcha Nathan Grünburg, grandfather Aryeh Goldstein, and Aron Engel.

This proves to me he must have been rabbinically qualified.With the war over, more children were born and Leopold balanced his life working with different animal skins (furs) while continuing to assist the rabbi and the Jewish community. Tragically, during World War II, in July 1942, Leopold, Gizella, and five of their 11 children were martyred by the greatest assassin of Jews of them all. I never knew them.

[1] Rabbinical seminary

[2] Marriage-match

[3] German in Hebrew script, not really Yiddish

[4] The word derives from the word *ogen*, meaning an anchor. Basically she was "chained" or tied down, unable to remarry. The status continues today, if a Jewish man denies his wife a Jewish divorce.

Reserve Rabbis in the
Royal Hungarian Army, 1915-1918

II. sz. melléklet

A Magyar Királyi Honvédség tábori rabbijai (tartalékos állomány) és szolgálatteljesítésük kezdete a hivatalos névjegyzékek szerint

The Hungarian Royal Army rabbis (reservists) and their service according to the official directories.

1914. évben:

Dr. Kelemen Adolf (1889)
Klein József (1891)
Deutsch Gábor (1904)
Löwinger Márton (1904)
Grosszmann Zsigmond (1906)
Friedmann Ernő (1909)

1915. évben:

Dr. Drobinszky Jakab (1898)
Goldstein Lipót (1903)
Löwinger Márton (1904)
Frankfurter Mór (1909)
Friedmann Ernő (1909)
Hirsch Leó (1910)
Lemberger Samu (1910)
Feldmann Áron (1912)
Schlesinger Sámuel (1913)
Dr. Kálmán Ödön (1913)
Schück D. József (1914)
Dr. Bande Zoltán (1914)
Müller Lajos (1915)

1916. évben:

vacat

1917. évben:

Dr. Drobinszky Jakab (1898)
Goldstein Lipót (1903)
Löwinger Márton (1904)
Frankfurter Mór (1909)
Friedmann Ernő (1909)
Hirsch Leó (1910)
Lemberger Samu (1910)
Feldmann Áron (1912)
Schlesinger Sámuel (1913)
Dr. Kálmán Ödön (1913)
Schück D. József (1914)
Dr. Bande Zoltán (1914)
Müller Lajos (1915)

1918. évben:

Dr. Drobinszky Jakab (1898)
Goldstein Lipót (1903)
Löwinger Márton (1904)
Frankfurter Mór (1909)
Friedmann Ernő (1909)
Hirsch Leó (1910)
Lemberger Samu (1910)
Feldmann Áron (1912)
Schlesinger Sámuel (1913)
Dr. Kálmán Ödön (1913)
Schück D. József (1914)
Dr. Bande Zoltán (1914)
Müller Lajos (1915)
Sonnenschein Éliás (1917)

Joseph GOLDSTEIN
d. 18 Nov 1918, Czechoslovakia
& Maria KOHN

WWI

Leopold (Lipot) "Aryeh" GOLDSTEIN
b. 11 Aug 1882, Szina, Slovakia
d. Jul 1942, Poland (Auschwitz)
& Gizella GOLDMAN
d. Jul 1942, Poland (Majdanek Camp)
m. 5 Mar 1907, Kezmarok, Slovakia

Jindrich "Chaim" GOLDSTEIN
b. 1 Jul 1909, Kezmarok, Slovakia
d. 10 Jun 1959, Los Angeles, CA
& Esther

Madeleine GOLDSTEIN
& ISENBERG

David Goodman

One Englishman who volunteered to fight...

Israel Reiss

and one who wouldn't!

Israel Reiss - 1916

David Goodman
and Sophia Bickler - 1915

One Englishman who volunteered to fight, and one who wouldn't!

Dr. Michael Anderson

This is an account of my Jewish forbears, largely of German origin, born and living in England at a time when that country was at war with Germany and their very contrasted attitudes towards doing their 'patriotic duty' as British Jews.

David Goodman, my mother's father was born in Leeds, England in 1891. Israel Reiss, a first cousin of similar age to my grandfather was raised by David's parents - my great grandparents, Hyman and Elizabeth Goodman, following the untimely deaths of his own parents.

Israel Reiss told his granddaughter, my cousin Marnie, that he couldn't stand to fight and so had 'deserted.' He would tell her no more of his war-time experiences. But I found record of Israel having joined the British Army as a youth in 1905 and going to France as a reservist with the regular troops at the very start of the conflict. He fought in many major battles between 1914 and 1916 and was invalided out of the War in 1916, spending the next two years recuperating in hospital from his wounds. For his bravery from the start of this bloody European conflict, he was awarded the 'Mons Star.' Yet Israel's willingness to fight Germans was despite his having maternal grandparents, Herman and Fanny Gutman who were from Germany and a German father, Marks Reiss, whose family had come to live in England from Leipzig in the 1860's.

David Goodman, my grandfather, in contrast resisted all patriotic pressure to volunteer to serve and only joined the fighting forces when he was conscripted into the British Army in 1916. He did what he could to evade danger, having himself employed in the 'Labour Corps' working in Leeds alongside his tailor father, Hyman, making uniforms for soldiers. Fearing that he might be sent into active service he contrived in August 1918 to have himself discharged from the Army 'as no longer medically fit,' maintaining that since childhood he had 'a constitutional heart weakness.' He is described in the 1918 Army records as 'honest and sober.'

My grandfather did indeed die from a heart attack – but that was in 1969 more than 50 years later. He used to say about World War I that 'no one needed to fight in that stupid war, you just had to know the right person to bribe to be out of it!' "Sober" he definitely was, but "honest" - I don't think so!

Doubtless as well as from his German father, Hyman, there would have been resistance from David Goodman's in-laws to an active fight with Germany since he had married my grandmother, Sophia in 1915 and her father, Jacob Bickler, was from Prussia and considered himself a German Jew.

There must have been so much of English Jews fighting German Jews in that great and awful conflict. Many of the Goodman and Bickler cousins would of course have been fighting in the trenches on the 'other side.'

I'd just conclude with acknowledgement that had my grandfather been killed in that 'war to end all wars,' the sad fate of more than a million young British men, I would of course not have been born! Also, that the Jewish Community in Leeds would have been deprived of the the benefit of my grandfather's legendary generosity. Thus David Goodman, for very many years after World War I, made employment for Israel Reiss and numerous other family members in the gaming clubs and restaurants he set up in Leeds and the Stray Hotel which he owned in Harrogate.

Honest & sober

British Army WWI Pension Records 1914-1920

Jack Herschkowitz

American fighting in France

Herschkowitz, Jack   1,708,138   * White * Colored
(Surname)   (Christian name)   (Army serial number)

Residence: _____ 249 E Houston St. New York   NEW YORK
          (Street and house number)   (Town or city)   (County)   (State)

~~Enlisted in N. G. N. Y.~~ *Inducted at New York N Y   on Sept 20 19 17

Place of birth: _____ Roumania _____ Age or date of birth? 27 9/12yrs

Organizations served in, with dates of assignments and transfers: ___ Co C 308 Inf to disch.

Grades, with date of appointment: ____ Pvt 1 cl July 1/18

Engagements:

Wounds or other injuries received in action: None.

Served overseas from † Apr 6/18 to † Apr 28/19, from † _____ to †_____

Honorably discharged on demobilization ___ May 9/19 _____, 19___

In view of occupation he was, on date of discharge, reported _____ per cent disabled.

Remarks: _____ Awarded French Military Medal; (Fr C De G)DSC
                              (with palm)

Form No. 724 1, A. G. O.   * Strike out words not applicable.   † Dates of departure from and arrival in the U. S.
Nov. 22. 1919.

New York, Abstracts of World War I Military Service, 1917-1919

65

Jack Herschkowitz

Barbara Hershey

Jack Herschkowitz was born in Iasi (Yassy) Romania in 1889. He came to the United States c. 1905 and lived in New York City and Great Neck, NY. He was a wholesale grocer in partnership with his brother, Herman and uncle Michel Lowenthal. They sold items like dried fruit and nuts. He married Sadie and they had two daughters Phyllis and Lois. Jack was drafted in 1917 and was part of a notable military action referred to as the "Lost Battalion" (not to be confused with an episode of the same name in World War II). He was awarded the Distinguished Service Cross, Croix de Guerre with Palms, Medaille Militaire and more. Allegedly his "German" language skills were at play although I'm quite confident that he spoke Yiddish, not German. Please see attached citations, articles and notices. It appears there was a movie made about this episode and a few of the characters, including Jack, played themselves. There is a picture of the poster for this 1919 film at this website:

http://silenthollywood.com/thelostbattalion1919.html
The website also includes the cast and advisors.

"The Lost Battalion"

Distinguished Service Cross Award for
JACK HERSCHKOWITZ

Home of record: New York New York

projects.militarytimes.com

Awarded for actions during the World War I

The President of the United States of America, authorized by Act of Congress, July 9, 1918, takes pleasure in presenting the Distinguished Service Cross to Private Jack Herschkowitz (ASN: 1708138), United States Army, for extraordinary heroism in action while serving with Company C, 308th Infantry Regiment, 77th Division, A.E.F., near Binarville, France, 29 September 1918. In order to obtain ammunition and rations, Private Herschkowitz, with another soldier, accompanied an officer in an effort to reestablish communication between battalion and regimental headquarters. They were attacked by a small party of Germans, but drove them off, killing one. When night came they crawled unknowingly into the center of a German camp, where they lay for three hours undetected. Finally discovered, they made a dash to escape. In order to protect the officer, Private Herschkowitz deliberately drew the enemy fire to himself, allowing the officer to escape. Private Herschkowitz succeeded in getting through and delivering his message the next morning.

General Orders: War Department, General Orders No. 13 (1919)

Action Date: 29-Sep-18

Service: Army

Rank: Private

Company: Company C

Regiment: 308th Infantry Regiment

Division: 77th Division, American Expeditionary Forces

Holdengraber and Echenberg Families

Rebecca
Echenberg

Claire
Echenberg

Sydney Holdengraber

The Holdengrabers and Echenbergs

Dean Echenberg

Sydney Holdengraber from Sherbrooke and Montreal, Quebec joined the Canadian Expeditionary Forces twice. The first time, when he was 15 years old, he went through training and was not caught for several months. He was immediately released from the service. He waited until he became of age and then joined a second time and he was accepted. He served overseas until the end of the war when he was released a second time.

Louis Thomas Echenberg and Samuel Echenberg, both from Sherbrooke, Quebec, also served overseas. Samuel was mentioned in dispatches for his service. He later went on to become Colonel and commander of the Sherbrooke Regiment. During the Second World War he was the highest ranking Jew in the Canadian Army.

Rebecca Echenberg was a nurse who served with the Medical Corps overseas. Claire Echenberg was also a nurse who served.

DUPLICATE

117th EASTERN TOWNSHIPS **ATTESTATION · PAPER.**   No. 748457

OVERSEAS BATT., C. E. F.

Folio.

CANADIAN OVER-SEAS EXPEDITIONARY FORCE.

QUESTIONS TO BE PUT BEFORE ATTESTATION.
(ANSWERS.)

1. What is your surname?	Echenberg.
1a. What are your Christian names?	Louis Thomas.
1b. What is your present address?	Sherbrooke. Que.
2. In what Town, Township or Parish, and in what Country were you born?	Ostropole. Russia.
3. What is the name of your next-of-kin?	Mrs. Passie Echenberg.
4. What is the address of your next-of-kin?	Ostropole. Russia. Prov. Volyn.
4a. What is the relationship of your next-of-kin?	Mother.
5. What is the date of your birth?	28th July. 1889. (Russ Cal.)
6. What is your Trade or Calling?	Interpreter.
7. Are you married?	No.
8. Are you willing to be vaccinated or re-vaccinated and inoculated?	Yes.
9. Do you now belong to the Active Militia?	No.
10. Have you ever served in any Military Force? If so, state particulars of former Service.	No.
11. Do you understand the nature and terms of your engagement?	Yes.
12. Are you willing to be attested to serve in the CANADIAN OVER-SEAS EXPEDITIONARY FORCE?	Yes.

*Canada,
Soldiers
of the First
World War,
1914-1918*

Sydney Holdengraber

Jacobson and David Families

My Latvian and Lithuanian Families

Postcard from Riga, Latvia to South Africa, 1915

My Latvian and Lithuanian Families

Bernie Isme

My Latvian Family in World War I

My grandmother was one of five Jacobson siblings. All except one had left Latvia for South Africa before the war broke out. The member of the family who stayed behind was Necha, known as Nanny, who married Meyer David and continued to live in Libau. A post card (page 70) from Meyer to my grandmother in South Africa came during this problematic time in Europe:

Riga. 4 August 1915.

We are already 4 months here… In Libau, everything is alright, all well don't wait from us any letters, you know how it is now. We hope to go soon home. Nanny and I send you all our best love and regards.

In January 1915, during World War I, German armies broke through the Russian lines and overran Poland, Lithuania and Courland. Libau, a strategic port, was one of the first places that they attacked, bombing the town with dirigibles. In 1915 Jews were given 48 hours to leave for the interior of Russia. In May 1916, the German army occupied the town. Meyer and Nanny would have gone to Riga to escape, just as in another war, nearly thirty years later, they once again looked for refuge elsewhere.

My Lithuanian Family in World War I

My Bene grandfather and his oldest sons had left Shavlan [Siaulenai, Lithuania] for South Africa before the war broke out. My grandmother, the girls and the youngest son were caught by World War I. They were sent to the Ukraine for the duration of the war.

This photograph of them was probably taken to send to the family in South Africa, probably just after the war. They left for South Africa in 1922.

David and Solomon Kastner

Austrian Army

Solomon, in his Austrian Army uniform,
and his cousin Moishe Kastner

David Kastner and Family

Merle Kastner

David Kastner, my grandfather, originally lived in Fratautii, a very tiny town eight kilometers from Radauti, Bukovina (Austrian Republic). He fought with the Austrian forces and was prisoner of war in Russia for six years. When the war ended, David came home to Fratautii. When he finally returned to his family, his eldest child Dora, then six years old, refused to recognize him.

His cousins, Moishe and Solomon Kastner, moved to Mannheim, Germany.

My grandfather David made a trip back to his home city, Radauti, Bukovina (then Austria) in 1914 to visit his family, but barely managed to escape the country as World War I was breaking out. He was forced to bribe officials to allow him to leave Austrian territory and return safely to Canada.

This 1926 photo shows my grandfather's nephew, David Kastner, with his wife, Rosa Rudich, daughter Dora, son Joel and daughter Jeanette "Nettie". David had been a prisoner of war in Russia for 6 years.

Hans Kelsen

Austrian Army and Ministry of War

Hans Kelsen
was born in
Prague in 1881.
Both military photos
were taken about 1915

Hans Kelsen

Anne Feder Lee

Hans Kelsen was born in 1881 in Prague. His father was from Brody, Ukraine and his mother from Jindrichuv Hradec, Czechoslovakia. They married in Vienna in 1880 at the Tempelgasse Synagogue in Vienna. Shortly thereafter, they went to Prague where he was involved in the plumbing business. About 3 years after Kelsen was born, the family returned to Vienna where his father set up a glass lamp factory. After World War I, Kelsen became full professor of law at the University of Vienna and served for some years on the Austrian Constitutional Court. He then became Dean of the Law School in Cologne, Germany but was forced to leave once the Nazis came to power. He and my grandmother came to the United States in 1940.

The turning point in my grandfather's career came with the beginning of the First World War and ended up having an important impact not only on the Austrian legal system, but also on legal systems around the world.

After his 1900 graduation from high school in Vienna, he (like many other Austrian high school graduates) joined the Austro-Hungarian army. He became a lieutenant in 1902. At the same time, he began studying law at the University of Vienna. In 1906, he received a doctorate in law and obtained the "Habilitation" (license to hold university lectures) from the Faculty of Law, University of Vienna in 1911. From then until World War I he pursued his academic profession with teaching, writing and publishing.

One week after the start of World War I, Kelsen was drafted (4 August 1914). However, since he had previously served in the military, had attained the rank of lieutenant, and came down with pneumonia, he did not have to serve on the front line. Rather, he ended up being assigned to office work, including some time at the *Kriegsfürsorgeamt*, an office overseeing the welfare of injured military personnel.

In October of 1915, Kelsen was transferred to the Ministry of War where he worked until the end of the war. There he gained the trust of the minister, Rudolf Freiherr Stöger-Steiner von Steinstätten (the last War minister of the Austro-Hungarian Empire) and became his personal adviser. In this position Kelsen drafted not only proposals for reforms of the army, but developed plans to reform the Habsburg monarchy (including ideas about constitutional reforms) that would take place once the war was over. Even though the plans worked on at the Ministry never came to fruition, his work did gain the attention of various individuals involved in academics and government/politics.

In 1919, he worked on drafting a constitution for the new country of Austria which came into being with the end of the war. Current scholars of Kelsen's work and life state that he drafted the document at the request of Chancellor Karl Renner. I happen to like a slightly different version told by my family --- that a memo was circulated asking for drafts of such a document and that the only person to follow up was Kelsen. In any case, a constitution based on his draft was enacted by the Austrian Parliament on 1 October 1920. That constitution ceased to exist in 1934 with the rise of the Austro-fascistic regime of E. Dollfuss (which was replaced by the German Nazi regime in 1938). The "Kelsen Constitution" came back into effect on 1 May 1945 and continues to govern the Austrian federal system today even though it has been revised/amended at various times.

Kelsen's draft (and the adopted Austrian constitution) included something quite new: a constitutional court that had the power of judicial review. This was based on the American experience but with a significant twist. U.S. Chief Justice John Marshall established, in the famous *Marbury v. Madison* case of 1803, the concept of judicial review, that is, the power of courts to strike down laws if they violate the Constitution. This made the courts the final authority of what was/was not constitutional even though no such power is specified in the U.S. Constitution. In contrast, the Austrian Constitution establishes a specific court to deal only with issues of what is or is not constitutional: *the Verfassungsgerichtshof Österreich* (Constitutional Court of Austria). There are now at least 70 nations around the world using variations of Kelsen's model for a constitutional court.

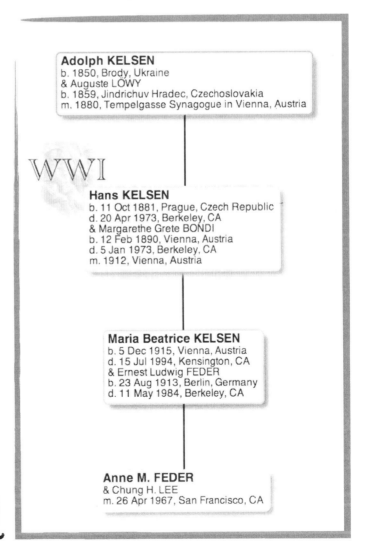

Adolph KELSEN
b. 1850, Brody, Ukraine
& Auguste LÖWY
b. 1859, Jindrichuv Hradec, Czechoslovakia
m. 1880, Tempelgasse Synagogue in Vienna, Austria

WWI

Hans KELSEN
b. 11 Oct 1881, Prague, Czech Republic
d. 20 Apr 1973, Berkeley, CA
& Margarethe Grete BONDI
b. 12 Feb 1890, Vienna, Austria
d. 5 Jan 1973, Berkeley, CA
m. 1912, Vienna, Austria

Maria Beatrice KELSEN
b. 5 Dec 1915, Vienna, Austria
d. 15 Jul 1994, Kensington, CA
& Ernest Ludwig FEDER
b. 23 Aug 1913, Berlin, Germany
d. 11 May 1984, Berkeley, CA

Anne M. FEDER
& Chung H. LEE
m. 26 Apr 1967, San Francisco, CA

Jack Lebo

U.S. Navy Air Service in France

Jack with his plane, *Jenny*

Jack Lebo (Lebowitz)

Natalie Lebo Hamburg
Andi Hamburg Jacoby.

Jack began life in Bergen County N.J., in 1899, where he went to school just long enough to learn the basic ABC's. World War I broke out and he enlisted on 13 March 1917 at Ft. Slocum, N.Y. Since he reported that he was an auto mechanic in civilian life, they assigned him (rather quickly) to the Air Service. As he told the story, the "service" consisted of a few planes made of balsa wood, struts and a fabric chassis. There were two pilots – Billy Mitchell and his brother, John! My father, Jack, was assigned to be their mechanic and fly (not as a pilot) with one or the other- as the mechanic on board.

When they were sent overseas to France, their missions were only reconnaissance over the enemy lines. He often told the story of taking a few bricks with them and throwing them down at the enemy. Of course, he would remind us that weight had to be watched and not too many bricks could be loaded into the plane. Did they wear white silk scarves... YES! Wouldn't fly without it!

The Air Service became part of the Navy for a while because they needed the ships to take them home after the war. They were only capable of flying a very short distance. Once back in the States, and many years later, the Air Service was named the U.S. Air Corps. The rest is history.

Jack got the love of flying then and although he returned to civilian life in 1920, he re-enlisted in 1923. Then they let him fly… still wearing white silk scarves!

G. H. Q.
AMERICAN EXPEDITIONARY FORCES,

GENERAL ORDERS}
No. 38-A. }

FRANCE, *February 28, 1919.*

MY FELLOW SOLDIERS:

Now that your service with the American Expeditionary Forces is about to terminate, I can not let you go without a personal word. At the call to arms, the patriotic young manhood of America eagerly responded and became the formidable army whose decisive victories testify to its efficiency and its valor. With the support of the nation firmly united to defend the cause of liberty, our army has executed the will of the people with resolute purpose. Our democracy has been tested, and the forces of autocracy have been defeated. To the glory of the citizen-soldier, our troops have faithfully fulfilled their trust, and in a succession of brilliant offensives have overcome the menace to our civilization.

As an individual, your part in the world war has been an important one in the sum total of our achievements. Whether keeping lonely vigil in the trenches, or gallantly storming the enemy's stronghold; whether enduring monotonous drudgery at the rear, or sustaining the fighting line at the front, each has bravely and efficiently played his part. By willing sacrifice of personal rights; by cheerful endurance of hardship and privation; by vigor, strength and indomitable will, made effective by thorough organization and cordial co-operation, you inspired the war-worn Allies with new life and turned the tide of threatened defeat into overwhelming victory.

With a consecrated devotion to duty and a will to conquer, you have loyally served your country. By your exemplary conduct a standard has been established and maintained never before attained by any army. With mind and body as clean and strong as the decisive blows you delivered against the foe, you are soon to return to the pursuits of peace. In leaving the scenes of your victories, may I ask that you carry home your high ideals and continue to live as you have served—an honor to the principles for which you have fought and to the fallen comrades you leave behind.

It is with pride in our success that I extend to you my sincere thanks for your splendid service to the army and to the nation.

Faithfully,

John J. Pershing,

Commander in Chief,

OFFICIAL:
ROBERT C. DAVIS,
    Adjutant General.

Copy furnished to *Jack Lebowitz*

S. M. Beach

2nd Lieut. Inf.

Commanding.

82

Honorable Discharge from The United States Army

JUL 8 - 1925

This soldier having been
enlisted, re-enlisted at Fort
MacArthur, Calif.

F. Richards

Recruiting Officer

TO ALL WHOM IT MAY CONCERN:

This is to Certify, That* _____ Jack Sebrowitz _____

the armed Private 1st Class 7th Obs Sqdn A. S. Crissey Field C. S.

THE UNITED STATES ARMY, as a TESTIMONIAL OF HONEST AND FAITHFUL

SERVICE, is hereby HONORABLY DISCHARGED from the military service of the

Purchase, under the prov of sect III, a.R. 615   60.

UNITED STATES by reason of ‡ per letter Hq. 2 Corps Area Nov. 27, 1923

Said _____ Jack Sebrowitz _____ was born

in _____ Jersey City _____, in the State of _____ New Jersey _____

When enlisted he was 26 years of age and by occupation a Machinist

He had Brown eyes, Black hair, Dark complexion, and

was ___5___ feet _10½_ inches in height.

Given under my hand at Fort Hamilton   N.Y. _____ this

3rd day of _Dec_, one thousand nine hundred and twenty three.

Theodore K Spencer

Major Infantry D. O. S.

Executive Officer   Commanding

Form No. 525, A. G. O.
Oct. 9-18.

1—4164

* Insert name, Christian name first; e. g., "John Doe."
† Insert Army serial number, grade, company and regiment or arm or corps or department; e. g., "1,620,302"; "Corporal,
Company A, 1st Infantry"; "Sergeant, Quartermaster Corps"; "Sergeant, First Class, Medical Department."
‡ If discharged prior to expiration of service, give number, date, and source of order or full description of authority therefor.

Julius Leburg

German soldier perished
in the battle at Verdun
2 June 1916

Julius Leburg

Barbara Algaze

My grandfather, Julius Leburg, was born in May of 1876 in Strassbourg, Alsace, France, when it was part of Germany and was called Straßburg, Elsaß-Lothringen, Germany.

As early as 1901 he was married and living in Berlin, Germany. His only son was born in Berlin in 1903. In 1910 he had his own business with a partner, selling furniture and antiques. When World War I began he was already in his late 30's but he signed up to defend his country.

He was killed on 2 June 1916 at the Battle of Verdun, very close to where he was born. His son was 13 years old when he was killed. On 25 Jan 1942 the Nazis rounded up his widow and her sister and shipped them off to the Riga Concentration Camp in Latvia. In spite of her son's pleas, she had refused to leave Berlin because she could not believe that the Germans would harm the widow of a War Hero.

There is no specific burial place where my grandfather's remains rest, however, his name is mentioned on the very bottom of his parents joint tombstone, which is located in the Jewish section of Bergfriehof Cemetery on Rohrbacher Strasse in Heidelberg, Germany.

Herman Lehman

Jewish Legion in Palestine

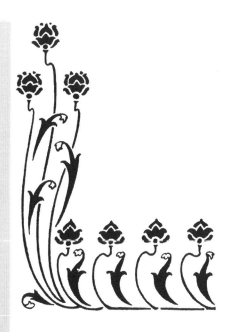

Herman Lehman -The Jewish Legion

Jeanette Shelburne

During World War I my grandfather, Herman Lehman, inspired by the vision of a Jewish homeland, enlisted in the Jewish Legion, a special unit of the British Army that fought the Ottoman Turks in Palestine. These 10,000 volunteers, many of whom were recent refugees from pogroms or forced military conscription, were proud to be part of the first Jewish fighting force in 2,000 years.

Herman was born in Malech, (now in Belarus) in 1897 and immigrated to Canada in 1904. A few years earlier, his father and older brother had escaped the Russian military conscription from which few Jews returned alive. Reaching Canada, they roamed the countryside as peddlers until they earned enough to send for the rest of the family. There, Herman was picked on by the town bullies because he was small and Jewish. Always the fighter, adventurous and positive, Herman would not remain a victim. He loved to tell us the story about how one day, he told the biggest bully, "I'll meet you after school." Being so small, he endured a punishing whipping but wouldn't give up. Finally, his tormentor cried out, "Enough!" and so Herman won. "But, boy was I sore!" he'd recount with a proud smile. Afterwards he was accepted, and enjoyed sports, camping on the St. Lawrence River and horseback riding with his friends.

In 1911, the Lehman family immigrated to the United States and Herman went to school and work in New York City.   Then, on July 28, 1914 Britain, France and Russia declared war against Germany, Austria-Hungary and Turkey. Later that year Zionist activists, Vladimir Jabotinsky and Joseph Trumpeldor, promoted the idea of creating a military unit, comprised of Jewish volunteers to fight against the Turkish army in Palestine. By the end of 1915 over 500 volunteers were training in Egypt.   Britain was reluctant to empower Jews militarily, but as they were in need of soldiers to defend their vast Empire, they finally agreed to this plan. The first Jewish Legionnaires were disappointed that they were not deployed to Palestine, but sent to the Gallipoli front as the Zion Mule Corps, with the un-glorious mission of transporting supplies. Nevertheless, they fought with distinction, earning citations and decorations for their bravery.

During the negotiations preceding the Balfour Declaration in which Britain would pledge to establish a Jewish national home in Palestine, two Jewish corps were organized. Although the British military commanders were opposed to the idea, Jabotinsky pressed forward and in August of 1917, formation of the 38th Battalion of the Royal Fusiliers was announced, and deployed to Palestine. It was comprised of British volunteers and a large number of Russian Jews who believed that if they supported Britain in World War I, it would reflect favorably on their aspirations for a national home in Palestine.

Then on November 2, 1917 the Balfour Declaration was made public. This was a letter issued by the British government to Lord Rothschild and signed by the Foreign Secretary Lord Balfour, stating that "His Majesty's Government view with favor the establishment in Palestine of a national home for the Jewish people. . ."

The British forces needed more soldiers so they asked permission from President Wilson to recruit in America. He agreed.

Seizing the opportunity, Jabotinsky travelled to Canada and the United States where he delivered fiery recruitment speeches to fight for a future Jewish homeland. My grandfather was one of the 5,000 young men inspired to enlist. At the time he was a dental student, but as he humorously recounted, "It was lucky I joined up, because I would have made a terrible dentist." Herman joined the Jewish Legion in 1918 and arrived in Palestine with the 39th Battalion Royal Fusiliers commanded by Lt. Col. Eliezer Margolin.

The 40th Battalion of the Royal Fusiliers was added later, comprised mostly of Palestinian Jewish refugees. Included in the group were future leaders of the State of Israel, such as David Ben-Gurion, Levi Eshkol and Itzhak Ben-Zvi.

These warriors were instrumental in defeating the Turks in Palestine, notably crossing the Jordan River for the final offensive of General Allenby's army, liberating Jerusalem, and at the Battle of Megiddo, one of the final and decisive victories of the Ottoman front.

After the war ended, the Jewish Legion was demobilized by the Anti-Zionist British military administration, but the soldiers had successfully accomplished their goal of helping to cement the establishment of a Jewish national home. They also had gained valuable organizational and military experience, which would help them form the nucleus of the future Jewish army in Palestine, the Haganah.

Herman Lehman returned to New York in 1919 where he would eventually start a watch import business and become financially successful.   For the rest of his life, he fought for the welfare of his fellow Jews. He was able to save many Jews in Europe before the outbreak of World War II by sponsoring their immigration to the US with employment and enlisting his colleagues to do the same.   He was an avid supporter for the State of Israel, organizing and providing financial support.   Strongly committed to the Veterans of the Jewish Legion, he contributed and worked tirelessly to raise funds to build Bet Hagdudim (House of the Battalions) near Netanya, a memorial, museum, library, auditorium, archiving records, documents, relics and writings connected with the Jewish forces of defense and liberation. He visited Israel every year and proudly wore his Jewish Legion pin wherever he went. In 1961 he attended the official dedication of Bet Hagdudim along with Israeli leadership such as former Prime Minister, David Ben-Gurion, former President, Itzak Ben-Zvi, Vera Weizmann, widow of Chaim Weizmann, the first President of the State of Israel, and General Zvi Tzur, who was then Chief of Staff of the Israel Defense Forces.

Sigfried Löb

German Serving in France

Siegfried and wife Rose

Siegfried Löb

Doris Loeb Nabel

Born April 22, 1899 in Hainstadt am Main, Hessen, Germany, my father, Siegfried Löb (Loeb), lived a Jewish life in an often hostile environment. Considering the difficult political and social environment in which my father lived, I am not surprised that he almost never talked about his youth, and the aggressive Nazi hatred he later survived. Growing up with an older German father, I hesitated badgering him. He died at the age of 87, in 1987.

After finding a postcard photo of him in uniform, I wondered about his military involvement, having known nothing about it. Was he conscripted, or did he enlist? On the address side of the postcard, in his handwriting, were the words, "Frühjahr (Spring) 1919 in Lich, Oberhessen." My mother told me that he drove a supply truck in France during the war.

Imagine my amazement, and emotions, when, in 2009, my husband discovered some of my father's papers in several manila folders inside a flat cardboard box in our basement. In 1991, we had moved my mother, Rose (Odenheimer) Loeb, from New Haven, to which my parents moved from New York City in 1941 or 1942, to our home. My father, who discarded items from the past that he did not value, had retained some documents, many in a folder on which he wrote, "Für Doris". I am an only child; he must have known that his sensitive daughter would be interested in his life.

One booklet, his *Militärpak*, includes nine pages of rules and policies, and data about my father, the divisions, companies, and roles in which he served, and supplies he received. Here I learned that he entered the army July 16, 1917, and trained as a truck driver. The booklet also shows that he completed his service July 4, 1919. My mother also told me that when my father took the test to obtain his license in the early 1940s, he did not pass the first time because he could not understand all the English directions.

Another booklet I found, his *"Soldbuch"* (paybook), contains seven pages of details about him, his physical appearance, deployments, and payments he received.

Following his return to civilian life, he bred, trained, and showed German shepherds, selling at least one to someone in the United States around 1927. My father also started a lumber business with his younger brother, Isidore, which they lost due to Nazi policies forbidding frequenting a Jewish business, and then not allowing Jews to own businesses.

My father bore the name of the famous Germanic hero of the *Niebelungenlied*, Siegfried, also son of a Sigmund. After serving in the German army in World War I, the Nazis picked him up on Kristallnacht in 1938, incarcerating him in Buchenwald. Sadly ironic.

Jacob Marateck

Russian
Soldier

Jacob Marateck

Anita Marateck Wincelberg's account
in
The Accidental Anarchist
Bryna Kranzler

In 1905, during the Russo-Japanese War, a Jewish soldier (and later officer) named Jacob Marateck began documenting the many ways the Czar had let down his own people. This was his rationale for wanting to overthrow the Czar. Marateck was sentenced to death three times (which he escaped), sent to a forced labor camp in Siberia (from which he also escaped), and fled to the United States--to Shenandoah, PA, where two of his brothers who had preceded him ran a haberdashery.

Marateck worked to raise money to bring his family over from Poland, but before he could do so, the Great War broke out. Following is a chilling account by Jacob Marateck's daughter, Anita Marateck Wincelberg, of what happened to her family when they got stuck in Poland during the War.

In the *"goldeneh medina,"* my father started out as a peddler, going door-to-door with what he hoped was useful merchandise. Just off the boat and not yet familiar with his new language, he was advised that, if asked a question, he should reply with the only English sentence he knew: "Look in the basket."

He worked hard and saved enough money to send steamship tickets to my mother but they never arrived; someone at the post office had stolen them. Undeterred, my father worked even harder to earn money for replacements, but before those tickets arrived, the Great War had broken out; my mother and the children were trapped in Poland until it ended.

During this time, a terrible blow struck. My brother, Chaim Mordechai, became ill. As there was no doctor in Vishogrod, Poland, my mother took the children to the train station to travel to another town that had a doctor. Despite her pleas, the railway guards refused to let them board. In a phrase that was all too prescient, one of the guards said, "We will get rid of all of you Jews. And if we don't finish the job, our sons and grandsons will."

Eventually, probably as a result of scraping together enough money for bribes, they were permitted to travel to the next town, but it was too late: my brother died of tuberculosis. He was four-and-a-half years old.

It took some time before my mother and two daughters were finally able to travel to America. By the time they arrived at Ellis Island, my sister no longer recognized the man she was told was her father, and initially would have nothing to do with him. And my mother, who had been robust and healthy, had developed a serious heart condition. Every Friday before sundown, when she lit the *Shabbos* candles, she cried for the little son she had lost, the brother I never knew.

I was two-and-a-half years old when my family moved to New York. The mines in Shenandoah had failed, and with the loss of those jobs, the general store that my parents ran lost its customers.
. . .

The Depression also gave my father time to finish documenting his experiences that he had begun writing about during the war. Over the course of twenty years, he filled twenty-eight notebooks with tales of his adventures, including serving as a bodyguard for Czar Nicholas II, whom he later wanted to overthrow; and about how conscripts needed to pretend fierce loyalty to the Czar, even going so far as to kiss the portrait of Czarina Alexandra, which hung in the barracks.

With help I spent many years translating [my father's] notebooks from Yiddish into English, and transformed them into stories. What was particularly challenging was making sure that the translation preserved and reflected my father's unique voice and humorous outlook on even the most horrendous circumstances. It was his sense of humor and unique perspective that helped him survive and make his stories so compelling.

In 1976, we published stories from the first twelve of the twenty-eight notebooks as The Samurai of Vishogrod (*Jewish Publication Society*).

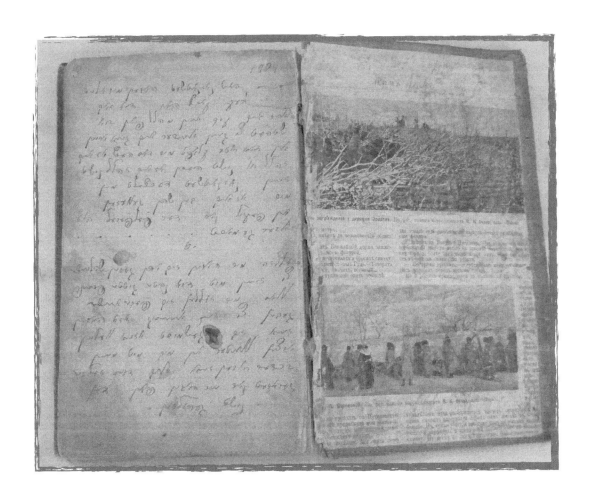

Alex Isaac Massion

U.S. Army Cavalry

Alex Massion (standing) and cousin Frank Prilook (seated) in both photos

Alex Isaac Massion

Andrea Massion

Alex Isaac Massion was drafted into the U.S. Army Cavalry unit and was miserable during his basic training. His letters to the extended family farming back in Iowa Center Flats, Wyoming, were written in Yiddish on USO paper and Alex lamented about missing his nieces and nephews, his elderly parents, and even his sister-in-law who read the letter out loud on her porch for all to hear.

Alex stopped in New York because he is seen here with his cousin, Bernard Prilook, also from or near Ananiev, Ukraine. The reunion warranted a studio photo to send to all the family. Bernard's brother, Frank Prilook also served in the army during World War I and returned to Cheyenne after the war.

Massion-Smaltz Family Tree

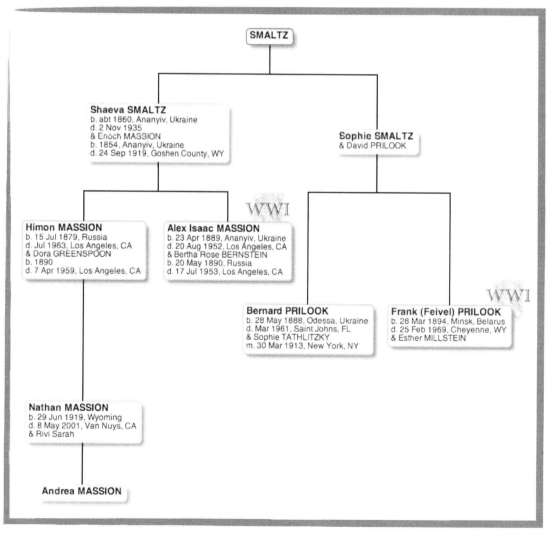

SMALTZ

Shaeva SMALTZ
b. abt 1860, Ananyiv, Ukraine
d. 2 Nov 1935
& Enoch MASSION
b. 1854, Ananyiv, Ukraine
d. 24 Sep 1919, Goshen County, WY

Sophie SMALTZ
& David PRILOOK

WWI

Himon MASSION
b. 15 Jul 1879, Russia
d. Jul 1963, Los Angeles, CA
& Dora GREENSPOON
b. 1890
d. 7 Apr 1959, Los Angeles, CA

Alex Isaac MASSION
b. 23 Apr 1889, Ananyiv, Ukraine
d. 20 Aug 1952, Los Angeles, CA
& Bertha Rose BERNSTEIN
b. 20 May 1890, Russia
d. 17 Jul 1953, Los Angeles, CA

Bernard PRILOOK
b. 28 May 1888, Odessa, Ukraine
d. Mar 1961, Saint Johns, FL
& Sophie TATHLITZKY
m. 30 Mar 1913, New York, NY

Frank (Feivel) PRILOOK
b. 28 Mar 1894, Minsk, Belarus
d. 25 Feb 1969, Cheyenne, WY
& Esther MILLSTEIN

WWI

Nathan MASSION
b. 29 Jun 1919, Wyoming
d. 8 May 2001, Van Nuys, CA
& Rivi Sarah

Andrea MASSION

Harry Mates

American Infantry Serving in France

4 June 1895, Eisiskes, Lithuania - 9 December 1973, Pittsburgh, PA

Harry Mates

Steven A. Morris

Below is the report of the action performed by my great uncle Harry Mates who was one of my paternal grandmother's older brothers during World War I.   He is memorialized at the Soldiers and Sailors Museum in Pittsburgh, PA. His action earned him the Distinguished Service Cross, the United States' second highest honor and the Croix de Guerre, France's highest honor. We have learned that the Medal of Honor was not given to "Jew boys" in World War I.

Private Harry Mates,
Company "H", 9th Infantry
(AS No. 246,456)
For extraordinary heroism in action near Blanc Mont Ridge, France, 3 October 1918. While acting as company runner, Private Mates carried messages under heavy shell and machine gun fire. When a machine gun nest caused a temporary halt in the advance of his company, he attacked the nest, capturing three prisoners. He assisted wounded men, applied first aid, and removed them through heavy shell fire to the dressing station. Home address: Mrs Ida Mates, 1321 Clark St., Pittsburgh, Pa.

WWI Military Cablegrams - AEF and War Department

The Pokorny Family

Stranded in Europe

John   Hannah

John Pokorny

Brad Fanta

Over 150,000 Americans were stranded in Europe at the outbreak of World War I, including my great-great grandmother, Hannah Pokorny Haas (photo) and her brother and sister-in-law, John (photo) and Clara Markstein Pokorny. According to Hannah's granddaughter, Constance Dannenbaum Levey, the Pokornys and Hannah Haas eventually returned to the U.S. in the hull of a merchant ship, a far cry from their luxurious steamer passenger ship accommodations on the outbound voyage.

The following excerpts from this New Orleans Picayune article highlight the anxiety of the time and places the Pokornys in Berlin at the beginning of the war.

3 Aug 1914, New Orleans Picayune
MANY ORLEANIANS TO FIND MEANS TO RETURN HOME
Washington Government to Look After Orleanians Who Are Abroad

New Orleans has special interest in the tourist situation caused by the war in Europe. This city supplies a large number of trans-Atlantic travelers every summer, and there are times when it does not seem that persons with money and credit are any better off than those of limited means. The tying up of the steamship passenger traffic between the United States and European ports, and of the railroads on the continent of Europe, has made Americans who are on the other side of the ocean realize this.

They not only are worried by their inability to get ships on which to return home, but are finding that they cannot even get money from this side, and unless they have gold with them are almost in the same position as if they were without means, except that the United States government and their friends at home are busy getting matters arranged that they may return, or be supplied with money should they elect to remain.

There has been great anxiety and uneasiness among Orleanians having relatives in Europe, but as President Wilson and Secretary Bryan have promised to take up the matter of sending ships to bring home those who desire to come, and to have orders for transportation home honored by European agencies, the funds being deposited with agents of the companies at the end, this anxiety is being relieved to a great extent.

Many New Orleans residents go to Europe every summer, and this year the number has been larger than usual. Many are in London and Paris, and many also are on the continent. The war declarations came so quickly that those in the interior had little warning, and these will have difficulty in getting to seaport, because the authorities have taken possession of all transportation facilities to move troops and supplies for the war. Americans in London are perfectly safe, and may return home as soon as the limited ship facilities permit, and in Paris and some other parts of France they may remain unmolested, but can travel to seaports and leave only under regulations. It is believed that the United States government within a few days will have chartered ships which will bring home those who desire to come. Congressman Dupre, who is home on a short leave from Washington, Sunday took up the matter for providing for the return of New Orleans citizens direct with the government at Washington, and learned that Mr. Wilson and Mr. Bryan had interested themselves.

Among the Orleanians in Europe or en route are many well known in society and in the business life of the city….

Mr. and Mrs. John Pokorny and Mrs. Hannah Pokorny-Haas are in Berlin;

15 Oct 1914 New Orleans Picayune

Mrs. Hannah Haas returned Tuesday from Clifford Springs, New York, where she spent a month after her return from Europe. She was abroad with Mr. and Mrs. John Pokorny, and toured with them from Southern Italy to Scotland and through Ireland.

Dr. Samuel H. Pogoloff

U.S. Army
Medical Detachment Serving in France

MENORAH SOCIETY

TOP ROW: D. Milstein, I. Milstein, Greenberg, Goldberg, Rothbaum, Lubovitz, Keller.
MIDDLE ROW: Sherman, Stekoll, Fagin, Bloom, Zinder, Lewis, Pogoloff, May.
BOTTOM ROW: Robinson, Cohen, Berry, Kahn, Byers, Futoransky.

University of Oklahoma 1921

Dr. Samuel Hirsch Pogoloff

Karen Pogoloff

Dr. Samuel Hirsch Pogoloff (born Polugaevsky), was born 20 Sep 1892 in Yasavok, Poltava Gubernia, Russian Empire to Hirsch Polugaevsky (aka Harry Pogoloff) and Rachel (Dubowitsky) Pogoloff. Dr. Pogoloff arrived in Galveston, Texas on 23 August 1911 with his father and brother Issak under the surname Pogulajewsky. His mother and eight additional siblings arrived in 1913. By 1916, he was a student enrolled at the University of Oklahoma and on 19 September 1917 he enlisted in the United States Army. Dr. Pogoloff was assigned to the Medical Detachment, 357th Infantry, 90th Division. The 357th Infantry was organized at Camp Travis, San Antonio, Texas as a part of the 179th Brigade, the Oklahoma half of the Texas-Oklahoma 90th Division in September 1917.

From the Regimental History of the 357th Infantry:

"On 20 June 1918 the Regiment sailed, and eleven days later arrived at Liverpool, England. The stay in England was no longer than it took to change boats, for on the following day the organization went to Southampton, from which it promptly proceeded to the Continent and assembled in the vicinity of the Aigney-le-Duc, France."

The 357th was involved in the following:

Battles:
St. Mihiel Offensive, 12 – 16 September 1918
Meuse-Argonne Offensive, 19 October – 11 November 1918

Other Engagements:
Villers-en-Haye Sector, 24 August – 11 September 1918
Puvenelle Sector, 17 September – 10 October 1918
Puvenelle Sector (Preny Offensive), 26 September 1918
Puvenelle Sector (Fme. Sebastapol Offensive), 23 – 24 September 1918

Dr. Pogoloff received the Silver Star for gallantry for action on 5 November 1918 (see citation below). He was hospitalized, as a result of being gassed during the action, from 9 November to 9 December 1918 in Beaumé, Aisne, Picardie, France.

Silver Star Citation Awarded for actions during the World War I by direction of the President, under the provisions of the act of Congress approved July 9, 1918 (Bul. No. 43, W.D., 1918), Private Samuel Hirsch Pogoloff (ASN: 2218091), United States Army, is cited by the Commanding General, American Expeditionary Forces, for gallantry in action and a silver star may be placed upon the ribbon of the Victory Medals awarded him. Private Pogoloff distinguished himself by gallantry in action while serving with the Medical Detachment, 357th Infantry, American Expeditionary Forces, in action at Villefranche, France, 5 November 1918, in going to the rescue of the wounded under heavy fire.

General Orders: GHQ, American Expeditionary Forces, Citation Orders No. 7 (June 3, 1919)
Action Date: November 5, 1918
Service: Army
Rank: Private
Company: Medical Detachment
Regiment: 357th Infantry
Division: American Expeditionary Forces

Dr. Pogoloff was discharged on 9 April 1919 at Fort Dix, Burlington, New Jersey. He returned to the University of Oklahoma completing his degree in 1921 and his residency in 1923. Dr. Pogoloff moved to New Jersey and on 14 July 1928 married Bertha Balinky, the daughter of Abraham and Sonia (Kutschuk) Balinky. Dr. and Mrs. Pogoloff have four sons: Boris Pogoloff, Joseph Maron Pogoloff, Paul Lee Powell, and Ralph Joshua Pogoloff. He had a successful medical practice in Somerville and Manville, New Jersey and was active in the New Jersey Veterans of Foreign Wars. Dr. Pogoloff was still having regular office hours until a few months before his death on 7 July 1981.

Dr. Aron Rein-Aronfy

Austro-Hungarian Military

Dr. Rein-Aronfy
and his bride Vilma Tropp

Portrait of Colonel Dr. Aron Aronfy
painted by his brother-in-law Mozart Rottmann

The Highly Decorated
Dr. Aron Rein-Aronfy

Susanne Spira

My grandfather Aron Rein was born on 30 May 1868 in Magyar Gyerö Monostor, in the county of Klausenburg in what was then the Hungarian part of Transylvania. Today it is known as Manastireni, in the county of Cluj, in Romania. The family later moved south about 120 km and lived in Karlsburg (today, Alba Iulia, Romania), where his father, Isaac Rein, was the manager of the Jewish Hospital.

No doubt the family's involvement with the hospital influenced his choice of career. My grandfather entered the Austro-Hungarian military service in February 1888, as a 10 year volunteer for the standing army followed by two years of the *Landwehr*[1], all to enable him to study medicine on an army state scholarship.

He began his studies at the Medical Faculty of the Budapest University, earning the title Doctor of Medicine in 1894. Concurrently he attended an officers' training course. His military evaluation papers indicate that he passed his exams with highest distinction. On completion of these in 1894 he was assigned as a physician to serve in an infantry regiment with the rank of *Oberarzt* (Lieutenant). Intermittently he would also be assigned to different other regiments and hospitals in the region.

In the late 1890s he married Vilma Tropp, daughter of Rosa and Pinchas Shmuel Tropp from Suceava, Romania. The wedding photo shows him in uniform, now with the rank of Captain (Regiment Physician). With each new assignment his growing family moved with him. In 1900 while stationed in Bialystok, his first son, Istvan was born; in 1902 his second son Antal arrived; and in 1904, my mother Elisabeth, born in Ungvar, completed the family.

From 1903 to 1914 he was primarily the chief physician of the army hospital located in Ungvar (now Uzhhorod, Ukraine).

When World War I broke out in 1914, chief physician Dr. Rein spent all his time on the front. Again he headed different field hospitals, but left his family behind in Ungvar. Over the years he earned several decorations, among them the Gold Military Merit Medal with Crown (1909) and for controlling and bringing a typhus epidemic to a halt, he received the Franz Joseph Order Knight's Cross (1916). The latter, was apparently the highest honor that could be bestowed. During the war he was again promoted, this time to major as *Stabsartzt* (Staff Physician).

In January 1915, two years after undergoing mastectomy, Vilma, my 38-year old grandmother, tragically succumbed to breast cancer. She, and her father, Pinchas Shmuel Tropp, are both buried in the Ungvar Jewish cemetery.

After the war, my grandfather continued his army service in the restructured Hungarian Army, attaining the rank of colonel. As a high-ranking officer he was asked to magyarize his German name. He decided to change it to the redundant sounding patronymic, Aron Aronfy[2].

Grandfather was 50 years old when World War I ended. Throughout, he managed to remain a practicing orthodox Jew and became an ardent Zionist. After the end of the war he considered sending his oldest son Istvan to study at the Technion in Haifa.[3]

My grandfather's high military honors and possibly his rank saved his life in the Holocaust. Unlike the German Nazis, the Hungarian Arrow Cross Fascists venerated their patriots and would not allow my grandfather to be deported.   He, his two sisters and his brother-in-law, Mozart Rottmann[4], lived "protected" under house arrest in their villa in Budapest at 84 Thököly Ut (Street) throughout the German deportations. Grandfather survived the war, but alas didn't live much longer afterward. On July 12, 1945, two months after VE Day (May 8, 1945), grandfather died at age 77.   He is buried in the orthodox Jewish cemetery in Budapest. His tombstone includes the Hebrew honorific מוה"ר (*morenu harav* = our teacher and rabbi) so I assume grandfather must have also been a yeshiva graduate.

Following Dr. Aron Rein-Aronfy's example, his only two grandchildren, I, as well as my only maternal cousin, Antal's son, Andras (Andrew) Aronfy became physicians. I think my grandfather would have been proud of the two of us: I, having completed not only my own military service as an officer in the Israeli Defense Forces, but also for having become a pathologist serving in another Jewish hospital (Cedars-Sinai in Los Angeles, California).   My late cousin Andrew also served in the US army and practiced pediatrics for many years in Maryland.

[1] A separate component of the standing army, functioning to assist the army & maintain order during war, and if necessary maintain order in peacetime.

[2] Meaning Aronson. He was granted the honorific Y at the end rather than I. this is somewhat similar to 'von' in German connoting higher societal standing. My Grandfather was named Aron (Aharon) after his grandfather.

[3] Opened in 1912

[4] Genre painter and portraitist, member of the Budapest Academy of Art.

Rein-Aronfy Family Tree

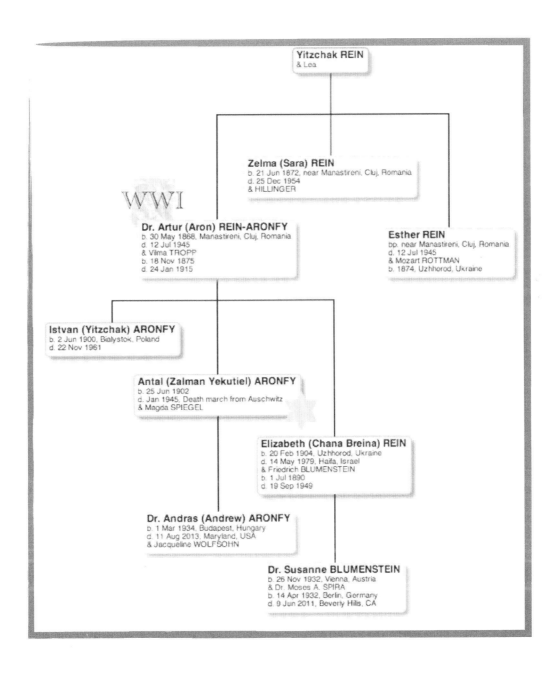

Yitzchak REIN
& Lea

Zelma (Sara) REIN
b. 21 Jun 1872, near Manastireni, Cluj, Romania
d. 25 Dec 1954
& HILLINGER

WWI

Dr. Artur (Aron) REIN-ARONFY
b. 30 May 1868, Manastireni, Cluj, Romania
d. 12 Jul 1945
& Vilma TROPP
b. 18 Nov 1875
d. 24 Jan 1915

Esther REIN
bp. near Manastireni, Cluj, Romania
d. 12 Jul 1945
& Mozart ROTTMAN
b. 1874, Uzhhorod, Ukraine

Istvan (Yitzchak) ARONFY
b. 2 Jun 1900, Bialystok, Poland
d. 22 Nov 1961

Antal (Zalman Yekutiel) ARONFY
b. 25 Jun 1902
d. Jan 1945, Death march from Auschwitz
& Magda SPIEGEL

Elizabeth (Chana Breina) REIN
b. 20 Feb 1904, Uzhhorod, Ukraine
d. 14 May 1979, Haifa, Israel
& Friedrich BLUMENSTEIN
b. 1 Jul 1890
d. 19 Sep 1949

Dr. Andras (Andrew) ARONFY
b. 1 Mar 1934, Budapest, Hungary
d. 11 Aug 2013, Maryland, USA
& Jacqueline WOLFSOHN

Dr. Susanne BLUMENSTEIN
b. 26 Nov 1932, Vienna, Austria
& Dr. Moses A. SPIRA
b. 14 Apr 1932, Berlin, Germany
d. 9 Jun 2011, Beverly Hills, CA

Lionel Rosebourne

Royal Navy Air Service Pilot

2 May 1891, Tredegar, Wales -
25 Apr 1970, North Vancouver, Canada

Name.	Corps.	Rank.	Regtl. No.
ROSENBAUM M Ⓜ	Monmouth R. 1/2 ─ ─ ─ ─	Sjt Lieut x	2298
Lawrence C Ⓑ B			

Medal.	Roll.	Page	Remarks On R.& F. Roll J/1/105 ᴮᵀ 2036
VICTORY Monmouth R. X OFF/167		66	Commn. Mon R. 7.1.16
BRITISH ─ ─		─ ─	X Decᵈ 12.4.18
15 STAR	J/1/14 Bᴴ	890	IVX/9645 df 30.11.22 NW/7/1976
			+ Initial
			Ⓑ Surname Amended auth. min. 7 NW/7/19761.
•			
Theatre of War first served in	1.		X
Date of entry therein	13.2.15		X NW/7/19761 K. 1380

Correspondence.

Address. Mrs. Rosenbaum 55. Church Street Tredegar.

E.1995. (1245 W½. W 2884—R.P. 6267 1,000m. 17/12/20, E. 6982.

British Army
World War I
Medal Rolls Index Cards, 1914-1920

Lionel Rosebourne

Paul Silverstone

My uncle, Lionel Rosebourne, joined the Royal Navy and was appointed a Flight Sub-Lieutenant at the Naval Air Station at Calshot in August 1917. Calshot was known for its role in the development of aircraft and flying boats. He was one of few Jews, perhaps the only one, in the Royal Naval Air Service. It was there that he received his flight training, and unfortunately crashed in the English Channel.

He was born on 2 May 1891 in Tredegar, Wales, as Lionel Rosenbaum, son of Solomon Rosenbaum and Brenda Brinetta Mittenthal.

Solomon was born in 1856 in Poland as was his wife and they married there prior to 1875. They emigrated to Britain and settled in Bedwellty, Wales, where their first child Bella was born in 1880. She was followed by nine more children all born in Wales. Solomon owned a pawnbroker's shop in Tredegar with a sign "Established 1881." Lionel was a bright student and was the first Jew to win a scholarship at the Intermediate School in Tredegar.

In August 1911, a current of anti-Semitism broke out in violence in Tredegar culminating in a riot. It was probably this event that caused Lionel to emigrate to Canada, and he arrived in Montreal on 13 Oct 1912 on the *S.S. Tunisian*. He was living in Winnipeg, Manitoba, when the war started in 1914.

He voluntarily returned to Britain and joined the Royal Navy, as a Flight Sub-Lieutenant in the Royal Naval Air Service. In January 1918 he returned to Winnipeg, and in March 1920 married my aunt Edith Finkelstein. For many years they lived in London, Lionel was a buyer at London fur auctions and made annual business trips to Winnipeg.

With the advent of war in 1939, the family left England and arrived in Montreal in June 1940, just after Dunkirk. Lionel lived in Winnipeg and Vancouver until he died in April 1970, age 78.

His younger brother, Lawrence Braham Rosenbaum, Lieutenant, 1st/2nd Bn., Monmouthshire Regiment, died of wounds 17 Apr 1918 received in action in Flanders. He had previously been badly wounded in 1915. Another brother Monty, also served as a sergeant in a Canadian Signaling Company.

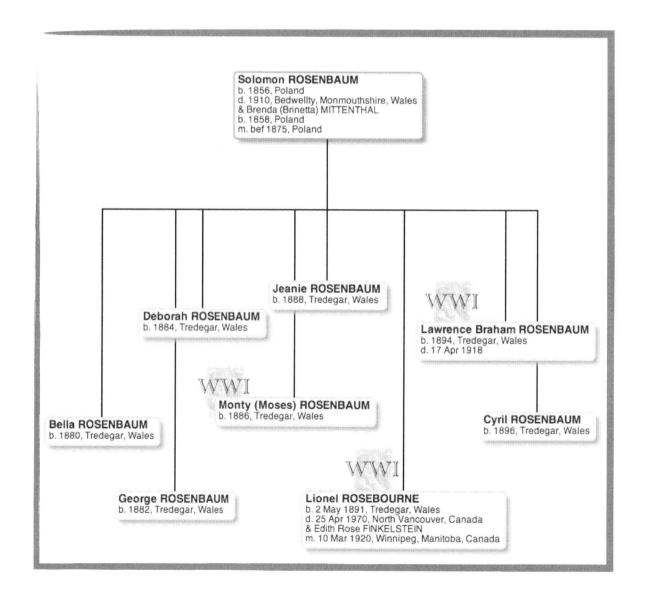

Harry and Louis Rosen

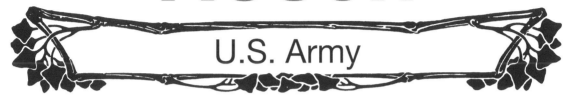

U.S. Army

Harry Rosen
US Army Infantry in France

Louis Rosen

Harry and Louis Rosen

Lois Rosen

Hirsch and Leib Rozinko were born in Daugavpils, Latvia (then Dvinsk, Russia). Hirsch (Harry) sailed to the U.S. to join his sister in 1908. His brother Leib (Louis) arrived in 1914. Both Rosen brothers were drafted into the U.S. Army in World War I. Louis was a musician and was assigned to play in the 212th Engineers' Band. He was a violinist by training, but band musicians were given woodwind or brass instruments to play. Harry was sent to France to fight, and family says he was never the same when he returned. They referred to him as "Harry who was gassed in the war".

Harry wrote on the *U.S. World War I Jewish Servicemen Questionnaires, 1918-1921* (see next page) that he suffered the effects of mustard gas 18 October 1918 and was sent to Allerey Hospital at Saône-et-Loire. He returned to the U.S., married, and had 4 sons. His sons changed their name to Roston. Harry died in 1962 in New Haven, CT. Louis married and had 3 sons. He died in Brooklyn, NY in 1981.

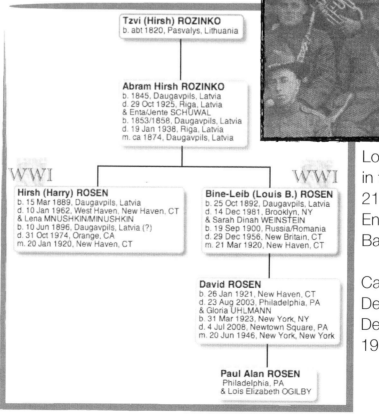

Tzvi (Hirsh) ROZINKO
b. abt 1820, Pasvalys, Lithuania

Abram Hirsh ROZINKO
b. 1845, Daugavpils, Latvia
d. 29 Oct 1925, Riga, Latvia
& Enta/Jente SCHUWAL
b. 1853/1858, Daugavpils, Latvia
d. 19 Jan 1938, Riga, Latvia
m. ca 1874, Daugavpils, Latvia

WWI

Hirsh (Harry) ROSEN
b. 15 Mar 1889, Daugavpils, Latvia
d. 10 Jan 1962, West Haven, New Haven, CT
& Lena MNUSHKIN/MINUSHKIN
b. 10 Jun 1896, Daugavpils, Latvia (?)
d. 31 Oct 1974, Orange, CA
m. 20 Jan 1920, New Haven, CT

WWI

Bine-Leib (Louis B.) ROSEN
b. 25 Oct 1892, Daugavpils, Latvia
d. 14 Dec 1981, Brooklyn, NY
& Sarah Dinah WEINSTEIN
b. 19 Sep 1900, Russia/Romania
d. 29 Dec 1956, New Britain, CT
m. 21 Mar 1920, New Haven, CT

David ROSEN
b. 26 Jan 1921, New Haven, CT
d. 23 Aug 2003, Philadelphia, PA
& Gloria UHLMANN
b. 31 Mar 1923, New York, NY
d. 4 Jul 2008, Newtown Square, PA
m. 20 Jun 1946, New York, New York

Paul Alan ROSEN
Philadelphia, PA
& Lois Elizabeth OGILBY

Louis Rosen in the 212th Engineers' Band

Camp Devens, MA December 1918

WAR RECORD OF AMERICAN JEWS

SEP 4 1919

CASUALTIES

Compiled by the Office of War Records of the American Jewish Committee, in cooperation
with the Jewish Welfare Board and other leading organizations, as a permanent memorial
of Jewish Service in the World War and as a contribution to American and Jewish history.

1. Name in Full _Harry Rosen_
2. Present Service or Business Address _31 Church St_
3. Legal Residence _16 Dow St. New Haven Conn._
4. Date and Place of Birth _Russia, 14 of March 1891_
5. Birthplace of Parents _Russia_
6. Education (if college or university graduate, give name of institution, date of graduation and degree obtained) _Russian High School_
7. Brief summary of civilian career before joining service

(CASUALTIES)

WAR RECORD

8. Full Name and Highest Rank _Pvt Harry Rosen_
9. Arm of Service (Army, Navy, Marine Corps, or Uniformed Auxiliary Service) _Army_
10. Branch (such as Infantry, Field Artillery, Medical Corps, Pay Corps, etc.) _Infantry_
11. Method of Entrance into Service (Enlisted, Enrolled, Drafted, Commissioned, or Volunteered) _Drafted_
12. Date of Entrance into Service _May 1st 1918_
13. Rank or Rating upon Entrance into Service and First Organization, Unit, Station, or Ship _Fourth Slocum_
14. Date of Leaving Service. (If still in service, so state) _June 1st 1919_
15. Highest Rank or Rating and Last Organization, Unit, Station, or Ship _1st Class Private_
16. Promotions or Official Recommendations for Promotion Received, with Dates Thereof

17. Length of Time Spent Overseas or Afloat, Counting Toward Service Chevrons _One Year_
18. Duties and General Location of Organization, Unit or Ship _Battle Field_
19. Participated in the following actions: _Alsace, Loraine, Molluvet Hill_
Molluvey Farm Trona Montague
20. CASUALTY: Killed in action or by accident; died of wounds or disease; gassed; shell-shocked; or taken prisoner.
(Please give circumstantial details as to nature of casualty, time and place, name of hospital, etc., etc. Copies of official documents are particularly desired.)
Mustard Gassed 10/18-18
Alleray Hospital Base 10.

Schneegurt Family

Lviv during the War

Schneegurt Family

Errol Schneegurt

My father lived in Lemberg [Lviv, Ukraine] during the First World War and recalled as a very young boy seeing a soldier lying in the street with his stomach blown open with his insides lying on the street. Nearby another dead soldier had his face partially blown off. He had stopped and stared, and was pulled away by his mother.

He recalled that after each battle the streets were littered with dead horses. With a lull in the battle people charged out of their homes with anything that could cut or chop. It seemed but a minute and there was nothing left of the dead horses.

The amount of food needed by the populace, under normal conditions, could not be met. The war stretched the supply to a critical state. Business could not operate and poverty reigned and famine raged. The non-Jewish population for both economic and anti-Semitic reasons boycotted the Jewish business. Pogroms raged and the pillaging of Jewish business and homes were common.

The following was translated from the Yiddish from statements my grandmother made, and were paraphrased by me.

My grandmother told me that the shortage of food in the city was so bad that people were starving in the streets. So when she heard that, that night, a mob was going to raid the Army storerooms in the city she decided that she was going to be a part of it. She was a fearless woman and went into action to relieve the food shortage affecting her family and the restaurant the family owned.

She said that, at the time, she had light hair and fair skin and it was easy for her to pass as a Polish peasant. As she put it a "Polack"! So she dressed up as a Polish peasant with a babushka on her head and accompanied by a man that worked in the restaurant (who was not Jewish) took a horse-drawn wagon and become part of the mob.

The mob which she was part of ripped down the barbed wired fences that surrounded the storerooms. Along with her helper she grabbed whatever they could and filled what they could of the wagon and ran off before the Army troops could get there to stop the looting.

This episode was a bit daring because she faced two dangers, the least of which was being caught by the soldiers. In her words "if the rest of the mob had known that she was Jewish and her helper was helping a Jew, they would have killed both of them on the spot." To share with a starving Jew was not in their character.

The only other reference to the war was that the family would go on summer vacations to a place called Zklo in the country. There a great uncle owned a large tract of land with several buildings on it. The true value of the property was in the mineral baths that were located on the grounds.

On the more sinister side there was a desolate spot at the back of the property that the children were not allowed to go to. It had something to do with the War and as my father put it, "there were things there that a young person should not see". He was under the impression that there were mass killings at the site.

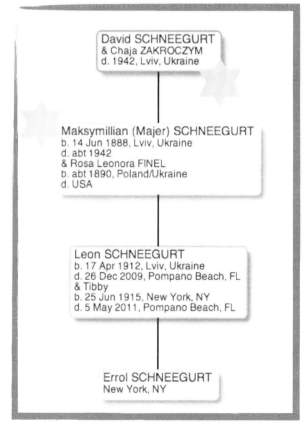

David SCHNEEGURT
& Chaja ZAKROCZYM
d. 1942, Lviv, Ukraine

Maksymillian (Majer) SCHNEEGURT
b. 14 Jun 1888, Lviv, Ukraine
d. abt 1942
& Rosa Leonora FINEL
b. abt 1890, Poland/Ukraine
d. USA

Leon SCHNEEGURT
b. 17 Apr 1912, Lviv, Ukraine
d. 26 Dec 2009, Pompano Beach, FL
& Tibby
b. 25 Jun 1915, New York, NY
d. 5 May 2011, Pompano Beach, FL

Errol SCHNEEGURT
New York, NY

Nathan
Schoenbach

Austro-Hungarian Sergeant -
Siberian POW

Nathan Schoenbach

Gabriella Zimmermann-Thaler

My paternal family originates from Galicia, before World War I part of the Austro-Hungarian Empire. In August 1913, my grandparents, Nathan and Fanny Schoenbach-Hechel, emigrated with their four children from Ustrzyki Dolne to Zurich, Switzerland. Due to Swiss law, which did not acknowledge Rabbinical marriages, my grandparents were regarded as not married and their children as illegitimate. As this was also the case for my grandmother's parents, she and the children had to carry her mother's family name, Thaler. My father, Moses Yitzhak, son of Nathan Schoenbach, was registered as Moritz Thaler.

My grandfather, Nathan Schoenbach, was born 12 March 1882 in Ustryki Dolne, Lisko. He was a *feldwebel* (sergeant) in the Austro-Hungarian Army. In Switzerland, in his civil life, he earned his living as a tradesman. Nathan and Fanny had been together just one year when an event changed everything in their lives.

On 28 July 1914 Austro-Hungary declared war on Serbia. Men at home and abroad were mobilized. Any man not appearing would be deemed a deserter and executed. Therefore my grandfather Nathan joined the army. When he reached the Eastern Front the war was fully involved. Unfortunately my grandfather was wounded by Russian fire, taken prisoner, and deported east. A postcard from him to his wife showed that he was a POW at the camp of Krasnaya Rechka, near Khabarovsk, 500 miles north of Vladivostok.

My grandfather could not be repatriated at the end of World War I (1918) because of the ongoing Russian Revolution. After having survived the five and a half harsh years of imprisonment, he travelled to Europe on a vessel provided by the U.S. Navy with the help of the International Red Cross. The ship left from Vladivostok in the spring of 1920. To avoid the mines in the Japan Sea, the ship sailed around Sakhalin Island, along Japan, to the Red Sea, and through the Suez Canal to the Mediterranean. The men disembarked in Trieste. In July 1920 my grandfather took the train to Zurich and was reunited with his wife and children for the first time again after six years.

My grandfather then went to the Zurich Town Hall to register, as was the law. There, he realized that his odyssey had not really ended. He answered the questions honestly about his birthplace (Ustrzyki Dolne), his nationality (Polish since 1918), his most recent residence (POW in Siberia), and his marital status (single). What he had not known was that Switzerland's laws had become very strict for foreigners coming from Russia. My grandfather was issued a deadline of 20 July 1921 by which he had to leave Switzerland. He asked for federal reconsideration of his case, but that was denied. He departed for Vienna, leaving his wife and children behind in Zurich.

My grandfather spent the following years in different places in Austria, Poland and France. Around 1930 the Swiss law changed and he was able to cross the border legally. He moved with his family to the small town of Baden. He had been wounded by the Russians - shrapnel lodged in his brain. This could not be removed surgically, and he occasionally suffered from seizures. He was only 48 years old, but could not work full time. He earned a bit of money as *shames* of the local synagogue in Baden, Switzerland.

Grandfather Nathan died 8 March 1960 in Baden, and is buried in the town's Jewish Cemetery. His Hebrew name was Nuchem ben Chaym Ha-Levi.

22 April 1919
Pesach
POW Camp, Krasnaya Rechka

Schoenbach Family Tree

WWI

Nathan (Nuchem) SCHOENBACH
b. 12 Mar 1882, Ustrzyki Dolne, Galicia
d. 8 Mar 1960, Baden, Switzerland
& Fanny (Feige Mirl) HECHEL-THALER
b. 4 Apr 1887, Ustrzyki Dolne, Galicia
d. 18 Oct 1974, Zurich, Switzerland

Sara Chaya HECHEL-THALER
b. 17 Feb 1909, Ustrzyki Dolne, Galicia
d. 30 Apr 1983, St. Louis, France
& Hermann (Zvi) SPRUCH
b. 4 Dec 1903, Kolomea, Galicia
dp. Strasbourg, France

Taube HECHEL-THALER
b. 20 Mar 1911, Ustrzyki Dolne, Galicia
d. 2004, Dijon, France
& Benno KLEIN
bp. Brzesko, Galicia
dp. Dijon, France

Jonas SCHOENBACH
b. 13 Feb 1910, Ustrzyki Dolne, Galicia
d. 19 Nov 1966, Zurich, Switzerland

Moses Isaac (Moritz) THALER
b. 25 Dec 1912, Ustrzyki Dolne, Galicia
d. 23 Sep 2000, Uitikon/Zurich, Switzerland
& Maria Maddalena MARTINI
b. 12 Sep 1908, Augsburg, Germany
d. 16 Dec 1979, Kilchberg/Zurich, Switzerland

Gabriella Giuseppina THALER
& ZIMMERMANN

Schwartz Brothers

Ignatz Schwartz

Ignatz Schwartz
& friend Harry Feiler were assigned
to Camp Hancock, near Augusta, GA

Schwartz Brothers

Sandy Malek

IGNATZ SCHWARTZ AND HARRY B. FEILER

My cousin Ignatz was born in Vitka, Hungary in 1890. He worked as a neckwear maker while he became a Yiddish teacher. He served in the US Army in World War I, from 16 July 1918 to 1 February 1919. He was never sent overseas, but served the entire time in Camp Hancock, outside of Augusta, Georgia. He appears to have been assigned to the Motor Garage, which would have been a huge Army mistake, as Ignatz was not particularly mechanical!

Serving with Ignatz was his lifelong friend Harry B Feiler, from Solotwina, Austria, born in 1894-95. Both were neckwear workers together in New York. Both were assigned to Camp Hancock, Georgia, but Harry Feiler was assigned to the base hospital. Harry Feiler served from 27 May 1918 to 4 Feb 1919, and was not sent overseas.

While Ignatz and Harry were at Camp Hancock, Spanish flu broke out. Records indicate that on 1 Oct 1918, flu cases jumped from 2 to 716 in a few hours, and by 5 Oct, Camp Hancock was quarantined with 3000 cases. By that evening, 50 soldiers were dead, and many more had contracted pneumonia.

Harry Feiler returned to New York and completed his medical degree at Columbia, Long Island Hospital in 1923. He was the well-loved family physician for the Schwartz, Klein and Malek families in the Bronx for the rest of his life.

DAVID SCHWARTZ

David Schwartz was the younger brother of Ignatz Schwartz, also born in Vitka, Hungary. He served in the Austro-Hungarian Army. He was a student at the Budapest Rabbinical Seminary, and the academic star of his family. He was killed at the age of 20. According to his published obituary,

> *"David Schwartz, student of the rabbinical seminary, corporal of the 5th Infantry Regiment, died a hero near Kolomea on March 18 [1915]. He was buried in the Jewish cemetery of Chofermitz [Chocimierz in Galicia]. The killer bullet reached him when he was running out from his shelter to help his captain who had been seriously injured."* *

SAMUEL [SAMU] SCHWARTZ

Samu was the younger brother of Ignatz and David Schwartz. No known picture of Samu exists. The story of his service in the Austro-Hungarian Army was written by his sister Sarah Schwartz Klein to brother Ignatz Schwartz in the United States, as follows:

> *"Poor Samu joined the army as a soldier on July 15, 1915 and went down to the front in October but in between he had been home on leave for 19 days, this was the last day we had spent together when we could not even create a thought of …, true, if I think back, when he was home, he was most of the time very dull, and I asked what the reason for that was, he took me and kissed me and diverted his speech to something else.*

> *"But as he went back I learned of the reason, when he had been home he had already known he was going to the front but he would not have mentioned a word about it to us…*

> *"He saw and knew how we were worrying about him and he did the same way as poor David that he always wrote only the best but we knew his state there very well…*

> *"Then he had been on the Front until August 31, 1916 and that is when the Russians took him as POW where he still spent one more year that is where he met his death, oh, my God!!!…*

> *"Both on the front and in the POW he had been suffering a lot, poor one…But there was almost no letter in which he did not mention you all, he was worrying about you,*

he thought you might have been interned. He could not write you from captivity because he did not know your address. I thought that you knew of each other. He was working in a factory there in Russia, there was a young man from Nameny with him, they had been real good friends and that one came home and told us his fate, told us that the work had not been so hard and it did not hurt Samu. He was in such good health that he had not been in and once as they were going home from work at noon and they went down to take a bath, as there was a great heat there, in a small river that was only as high as an apron, when poor Samu…

"They saw that his power was decreasing but they did not think he had a problem. Only when he went down under the water then they were running. But when he was found it was too late, they could not help. And then he was taken to the city and then he said that he had been buried as a Jew has to be buried. They immediately made him a Metsajni and a Mezajnes and then an old Jew was teaching…They could make it all from his own money. He, poor one, wrote us that he had received money from us three times but we only sent once so that is why I thought you might have sent it. This is how his life ended, leider, but you also have to accept God's will.

Oh, my God, if I think back when we heard this news, it is not even good to write about it…But for sure, our parents are so much heart-broken, Dad is so upset and you should see our mother, this all has made her older so much…" *

* Translation from Hungarian
 by Karesz Vandor
 info@hungarianroots.com

David Schwartz

Schwartz Family Tree

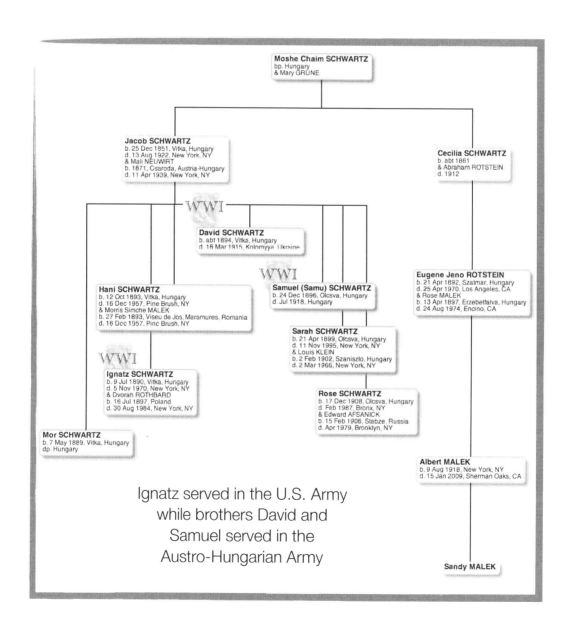

Moshe Chaim SCHWARTZ
bp. Hungary
& Mary GRUNE

Jacob SCHWARTZ
b. 25 Dec 1851, Vitka, Hungary
d. 13 Aug 1922, New York, NY
& Mali NEUWIRT
b. 1871, Csaroda, Austria-Hungary
d. 11 Apr 1939, New York, NY

Cecilia SCHWARTZ
b. abt 1861
& Abraham ROTSTEIN
d. 1912

WWI

David SCHWARTZ
b. abt 1894, Vitka, Hungary
d. 18 Mar 1915, Kolomyya, Ukraine

WWI

Eugene Jeno ROTSTEIN
b. 21 Apr 1892, Szatmar, Hungary
d. 25 Apr 1970, Los Angeles, CA
& Rose MALEK
b. 13 Apr 1897, Erzebetfalva, Hungary
d. 24 Aug 1974, Encino, CA

Hani SCHWARTZ
b. 12 Oct 1893, Vitka, Hungary
d. 16 Dec 1957, Pine Brush, NY
& Morris Simche MALEK
b. 27 Feb 1893, Viseu de Jos, Maramures, Romania
d. 16 Dec 1957, Pinc Brush, NY

Samuel (Samu) SCHWARTZ
b. 24 Dec 1896, Olcsva, Hungary
d. Jul 1918, Hungary

Sarah SCHWARTZ
b. 21 Apr 1899, Olcsva, Hungary
d. 11 Nov 1995, New York, NY
& Louis KLEIN
b. 2 Feb 1902, Szaniszlo, Hungary
d. 2 Mar 1966, New York, NY

WWI

Ignatz SCHWARTZ
b. 9 Jul 1890, Vitka, Hungary
d. 5 Nov 1970, New York, NY
& Dvorah ROTHBARD
b. 16 Jul 1897, Poland
d. 30 Aug 1984, New York, NY

Rose SCHWARTZ
b. 17 Dec 1908, Olcsva, Hungary
d. Feb 1987, Bronx, NY
& Edward AFSANICK
b. 15 Feb 1906, Stabze, Russia
d. Apr 1979, Brooklyn, NY

Mor SCHWARTZ
b. 7 May 1889, Vitka, Hungary
dp. Hungary

Albert MALEK
b. 9 Aug 1918, New York, NY
d. 15 Jan 2009, Sherman Oaks, CA

Ignatz served in the U.S. Army
while brothers David and
Samuel served in the
Austro-Hungarian Army

Sandy MALEK

Harry Shankman

U.S. Army in France

Harry Shankman
(Hershel Krasnitzky)

Ronald I. Miller

My grandfather, Harry Shankman (Hershel Krasnitzky) was born in and emigrated from Kiev, Russia and his father died when he was a child. He served in the US Army during World War I and died from the effects of being gassed during a battle. In 1917 Harry was drafted and served overseas in the Illinois Army National Guard that was federalized. He served in Company "L" (4th Platoon) . . . of the 3rd Battalion . . . Of the 132 Infantry Regiment . . . of the 66th Brigade . . . of the 33rd "Prairie" Division. When Harry Shankman first arrived in France in May 1918 the Division trained with the British, then went to the front on rotating trench duty. A myriad of details concerning World War I is contained in a variety of military documents and unit histories that are available in libraries, online, and at the NARA military archive in College Park, MD.

From August 8 – 13th he participated in the Somme Offensive Operation. During this time, the 3rd battalion of the 132nd Infantry Regiment, including Harry's Company "L," who fought in the battle of Albert. During much of this time his company also rotated trench duty on the front lines. Harry Shankman's Company "L" had every officer killed or wounded; it was commanded by the Company First Sergeant until the objective had been reached. Harry might have been gassed during this battle; he died in 1949 from the aftereffects of being gassed. The battalion also captured

400 Germans. After the battle of Bois-du-Fays the 3rd battalion attacked the enemy in Buttneville [sic] and drove them to the north edge of town. Later, they received word of the armistice (Signed at the 11th hour, of the 11th day, of the 11th month of the year). During this last day of the war Company "L" suffered 1 killed and 6 wounded.

Solomon Herzl Turner

Austrian Army

Solomon Herzl Turner

Steven Turner

My father, Morris Turner, was born in Nadworna, Galicia in 1910. Whenever I would question him about the shtetl he wouldn't have much to say because he didn't remember much of anything about it. The reason for that is World War I. In the summer of 1914, just days before the Russians invaded Galicia, a suspicious fire devastated the town. The Jewish area was particularly hard hit. Many Jews became homeless and sought refuge in Stanislawow and Bohorodzcany.

My grandfather, Solomon Herzl Turner was called to serve in the Austrian Army. My grandmother, Zissel Scher Turner was left to fare on her own with five small children. I don't know if my family became refugees after the fire or later on in the war but I do know that they left Nadworna never to return.

NADWORNA.

Nadworna is a town in Galicia, and when the Russians invaded it they not only forced all the Jews, men women and children, to assist them in the work of attack on the Austrian lines, but set them in the place of greatest danger as a shield for the Russians themselves. The Jews were commanded to take up bags of sand and carry them into the firing lines to build up walls of protection for the Russian soldiers. They were driven into the fire by the knout and by Russian bullets, so that they were placed between two fires, and many of them died on the battlefield as if they had been soldiers themselves, compelled to help a cause which was that of the inventors of pogroms.

(1917) "Nadworna," The Open Court: Vol. 1917: Iss. 12, Article 9.

As my father was very young he had little memory of his time as a refugee. He remembered just a few stories that he told me and my sister as children. One was of the time the family sought refuge in a shtetl that was very religious. The elders of the town demanded that my grandmother shave her head if they wanted to remain there. My grandmother, although she was an Orthodox lady, refused and the family left the town. He also told stories of how hungry they were and he remembered vividly his mother at one time having to slice just a small piece of bread for her five children to share.

Eventually the war ended and the family settled in Vienna where my Grandfather joined up with them. My father grew up in Vienna. Sadly, a short time later the family became refugees again. Two World Wars and twice my father was a refugee seeking safety from a war.

Nadworna

Samuel Wiesenberg

U.S. Army Serving in France

Wiesenberg, Samuel   3,182,659   * White * Colored
(Surname)   (Christian name)   (Army serial number)   1

Residence: ___88 Lewiston St___ ___New York___   ___NEW YORK___
(Street and house number)   (Town or city)   (County)   (State)

*Enlisted *R. A. *N. G. *E. R. C. *Inducted at___ L^P 157 New York N Y on May 26/18

Place of birth: ___Younover Russia___   Age or date of birth: ___May 10/1893___

Organizations served in, with dates of assignments and transfers:
___Co L 2 Pion Inf to June 23/18; Co F 51 Pion Inf to___
___disch___

Grades, with date of appointment: ___
          Pvt

Engagements: ___

Wounds or other injuries received in action: None.
Served overseas from † ___July 26/18___ to † ___July 3/19___ from † ___ to † ___
Honorably discharged on demobilization ___July 9/19___, 19___
In view of occupation he was, on date of discharge, reported ___0___ per cent disabled.
Remarks: ___

Form No. 724-1, A. G. O.   * Strike out words not applicable.   ^ Dates of departure from and arrival in the U. S.
Nov. 22. 1919.

New York, Abstracts of World War I Military Service, 1917-1919

Samuel Wiesenberg

Jerome Wiesenberg

My father, Samuel Wiesenberg was born in Janow-Lubielski, Poland on May 10, 1893. He arrived in New York City on March 5, 1914 on the *Kroonland*, which had sailed from Antwerp, Belgium. When I was very young, I happened upon a World War I medal and other memorabilia that he had kept in a drawer in his bedroom. I inquired what he did in the war, and his only response was, "I won it!" My sister also remembered asking him what he did in the war and he replied that he got to France when the war was over, which I later found to be untrue. We never pursued that question when my father was alive. It took a lot of patience, time and research to establish the facts related to his army service history.

World War I records that I found indicated that in May 1918 he entered the United States Army. Serving in Company F, 51st Pioneer Infantry Division, American Expeditionary Forces, he took basic training in Camp Wadsworth, New York. At its completion, the troops left there for France on July 29, 1918, sailing on the *Kroonland* and arriving in Brest on August 8, 1918. Although he never mentioned it, it was quite a coincidence that he sailed to America and returned to France on the very same ship! But as previously stated, he provided very little personal historical information while he lived. Perhaps the experiences of his war time involvement were too horrible to remember, as it is with many returning war veterans today.

According to some other historical records, I found that Company F, 51st Pioneer Infantry Division took part in the St Miehl, Meuse-Argonne and Defensive Sector campaigns. Through my correspondence with the US Army Records Division in Ft Knox, I learned that his service in those campaigns was verified and that they will be sending me his replaced World War I Victory Medal with the three campaign bars attached.

After the Armistice was declared in November 1918, the 51st was assigned to the Occupation of Germany forces where found family photographs show my father in uniform, wearing the armband of the Military Police. The Army has stated that an Occupation of Germany Medal, which he should have been entitled to, will also be sent to me.

He returned to the United States and was honorably discharged in Camp Upton, NY on July 7, 1919.

As a result of an accident, my father suffered a stroke, and was confined to a Veterans Administration Hospital for a number of years, dying there in 1980. One detail I remembered was his telling me that the only fight he ever had was while he was in basic training. It was with a fellow soldier who attacked him in an act of anti-Semitism. I now regret not gleaning more information from him while he lived. I am sure he took many memories with him to his grave, that his family and others would have appreciated learning about. Hopefully, perhaps some future additional research may uncover more information some day.

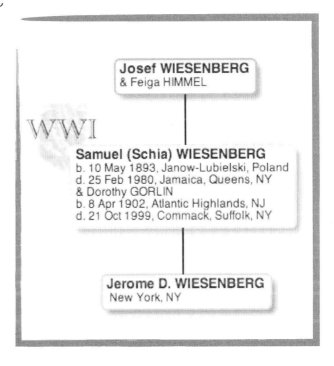

Richard Yoffe, MD

Captain,
U.S. Army Medical Corps
Allied Expeditionary Force
France

Uncle Doc -
Richard Yoffe, MD

Bill Yoffee

My great uncle (my paternal grandfather's half-brother) Capt. Richard Yoffe MD served in France with the AEF. He was attached to a British field hospital and was accorded the benefits of an equivalent British rank with all of its perks. Kopel Yoffe, his father, was my great grandfather and Esther Yoffe was Kopel's second wife. Kopel's first wife, Yetta, mother of five older sons and one daughter and who was my great grandmother died in 1890. Son Richard was born in 1892.

Richard Yoffe (born Reubin), Uncle Doc, was the youngest son of Kopel and was Esther's only offspring. He was also the only one in his generation to have a higher education and to become a professional. I always thought that his brothers Morris and Tobias helped to finance his education, which they could well afford, but when I read his father Kopel's will, I began to wonder how much help he needed from them. He attended medical school at Medico-Chi, which later became the University of Pennsylvania Medical School. He did not attend college first, because it was not required at that time, but he nevertheless acquired a liberal education on his own. He did his internship in Cincinnati and a residency at Tulane.

He became a full-fledged physician just before the United States entered World War I.

As a physician, he served as a U.S. Army Medical Corps captain in France. My father, with whom he was very close, remembered him in uniform, and that he was too short to wear the standard officers' boots. So he wore wrap-around khaki bandages below the knees. Notice the leggings in the photo of him standing in front of the ambulance.

He also had the distinction of holding an equivalent rank in the British Army while serving with a British Hospital Unit. This qualified him to have his own personal batsman (orderly). I've often wondered how some of his fellow British officers, many of whom came from the aristocracy, reacted to this little Jewish doctor, the son of a Russian Jewish American immigrant.

Letter of Appreciation
from
King George V
to the soldiers
of the AEF

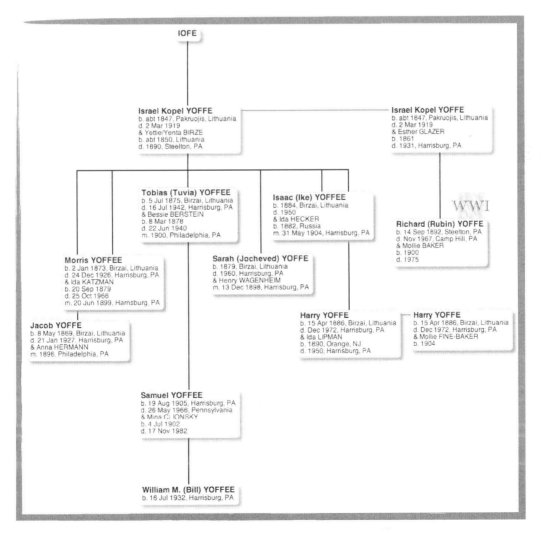

IOFE

Israel Kopel YOFFE
b. abt 1847, Pakruojis, Lithuania
d. 2 Mar 1919
& Yettie/Yenta BIRZE
b. abt 1850, Lithuania
d. 1890, Steelton, PA

Israel Kopel YOFFE
b. abt 1847, Pakruojis, Lithuania
d. 2 Mar 1919
& Esther GLAZER
b. 1861
d. 1931, Harrisburg, PA

Tobias (Tuvia) YOFFEE
b. 5 Jul 1875, Birzai, Lithuania
d. 16 Jul 1942, Harrisburg, PA
& Bessie BERSTEIN
b. 8 Mar 1878
d. 22 Jun 1940
m. 1900, Philadelphia, PA

Isaac (Ike) YOFFEE
b. 1884, Birzai, Lithuania
d. 1950
& Ida HECKER
b. 1882, Russia
m. 31 May 1904, Harrisburg, PA

WWI

Richard (Rubin) YOFFE
b. 14 Sep 1892, Steelton, PA
d. Nov 1967, Camp Hill, PA
& Mollie BAKER
b. 1900
d. 1975

Morris YOFFEE
b. 2 Jan 1873, Birzai, Lithuania
d. 24 Dec 1926, Harrisburg, PA
& Ida KATZMAN
b. 20 Sep 1879
d. 25 Oct 1966
m. 20 Jun 1899, Harrisburg, PA

Sarah (Jocheved) YOFFE
b. 1879, Birzai, Lithuania
d. 1960, Harrisburg, PA
& Henry WAGENHEIM
m. 13 Dec 1898, Harrisburg, PA

Jacob YOFFE
b. 8 May 1869, Birzai, Lithuania
d. 21 Jan 1927, Harrisburg, PA
& Anna HERMANN
m. 1896, Philadelphia, PA

Harry YOFFE
b. 15 Apr 1886, Birzai, Lithuania
d. Dec 1972, Harrisburg, PA
& Ida LIPMAN
b. 1890, Orange, NJ
d. 1950, Harrisburg, PA

Harry YOFFE
b. 15 Apr 1886, Birzai, Lithuania
d. Dec 1972, Harrisburg, PA
& Mollie FINE-BAKER
b. 1904

Samuel YOFFEE
b. 19 Aug 1905, Harrisburg, PA
d. 26 May 1966, Pennsylvania
& Mina CLIONSKY
b. 4 Jul 1902
d. 17 Nov 1982

William M. (Bill) YOFFEE
b. 16 Jul 1932, Harrisburg, PA